Schools on the Edge

Schools on the Edge

Responding to Challenging Circumstances

John MacBeath, John Gray, Jane Cullen, David Frost, Susan Steward and Sue Swaffield

Paul Chapman
Publishing

hinterland of major conurbations has stranded some adults and young people on the periphery of economic life and the schools they attend often sit amid the rubble of run down neighbourhoods, distanced from their surroundings by their values, traditions and frequently inflexible structures. Sometimes they are also physically distanced, on the outskirts of town, drawing young people literally and symbolically to a different place.

Education may be the route out of challenging circumstances if the will and skill can be found to navigate a path through the rigid conventions of schooling. Some young people, however poor the financial status of their families, are able to draw on a social capital in the home which provides momentum and support. There are others who, with no such legacy, still manage to surmount the obstacles of both school and social conventions to achieve beyond expectation. Others follow the line of least resistance into the twilight economy. Their uncelebrated intelligence is put to use on the margins of the law, lured over the edge into scraping a living by whatever means and sometimes criminal activity, what Manuel Castells has tellingly described as 'perverse integration', the back door entry to becoming accepted and achieving success (Castells, 2000: 74).

Those who teach these young people also come from a different place. The neighbourhoods these teachers visit on a daily basis are rarely the ones they would choose to live in or whose lifestyle they would choose to emulate. It is that very ability to choose that separates most teachers from those they teach. And it is the freedom to choose that distinguishes them from parents to whom governments proffer a choice of schools, as if choosing well might make all the difference between life on the edge and life in the mainstream.

Yet choice *is* exercised. It is often a rejection of the local school and the immediacy of its problems and the children who litter gardens and pavements with disused wrappers and Coke cans and inscribe their personal slogans on shop fronts and bus shelters. As these families choose schools in better neighbourhoods with 'nicer' children, they leave behind schools with a critical mass of parents and pupils who have less resilience or capacity to choose. They leave behind them as well schools which struggle to survive, year on year on the edge of viable numbers whilst attempting to meet the demand for public evidence that they are able to perform just as well as any other school, despite the unevenness of the playing field and the seemingly unyielding yardsticks of accountability.

Yet, however bleak the picture, there are schools in all countries which succeed in defying the odds, sometimes by statistical sleight of hand, sometimes by a concentrated and strategic focus on those students most likely to reach the bar and, in some instances, by inspirational commitment to deep learning across boundaries of language and culture. These schools are, in every sense, exceptional.

hinterland of major conurbations has stranded some adults and young people on the periphery of economic life and the schools they attend often sit amid the rubble of run down neighbourhoods, distanced from their surroundings by their values, traditions and frequently inflexible structures. Sometimes they are also physically distanced, on the outskirts of town, drawing young people literally and symbolically to a different place.

Education may be the route out of challenging circumstances if the will and skill can be found to navigate a path through the rigid conventions of schooling. Some young people, however poor the financial status of their families, are able to draw on a social capital in the home which provides momentum and support. There are others who, with no such legacy, still manage to surmount the obstacles of both school and social conventions to achieve beyond expectation. Others follow the line of least resistance into the twilight economy. Their uncelebrated intelligence is put to use on the margins of the law, lured over the edge into scraping a living by whatever means and sometimes criminal activity, what Manuel Castells has tellingly described as 'perverse integration', the back door entry to becoming accepted and achieving success (Castells, 2000: 74).

Those who teach these young people also come from a different place. The neighbourhoods these teachers visit on a daily basis are rarely the ones they would choose to live in or whose lifestyle they would choose to emulate. It is that very ability to choose that separates most teachers from those they teach. And it is the freedom to choose that distinguishes them from parents to whom governments proffer a choice of schools, as if choosing well might make all the difference between life on the edge and life in the mainstream.

Yet choice *is* exercised. It is often a rejection of the local school and the immediacy of its problems and the children who litter gardens and pavements with disused wrappers and Coke cans and inscribe their personal slogans on shop fronts and bus shelters. As these families choose schools in better neighbourhoods with 'nicer' children, they leave behind schools with a critical mass of parents and pupils who have less resilience or capacity to choose. They leave behind them as well schools which struggle to survive, year on year on the edge of viable numbers whilst attempting to meet the demand for public evidence that they are able to perform just as well as any other school, despite the unevenness of the playing field and the seemingly unyielding yardsticks of accountability.

Yet, however bleak the picture, there are schools in all countries which succeed in defying the odds, sometimes by statistical sleight of hand, sometimes by a concentrated and strategic focus on those students most likely to reach the bar and, in some instances, by inspirational commitment to deep learning across boundaries of language and culture. These schools are, in every sense, exceptional.

Introduction

This is a book about schools on the edge. It is, in part, a story of eight English schools living on the precarious edge between success and failure, but it is, in larger part, a narrative of schools and communities edging towards a common purpose and understanding of what is educationally important and achievable. The history of school education, wherever and whenever it has been written, provides accounts of schools in the centre of the social mainstream as against schools perpetually on the periphery. What brings them together is a common policy framework but their social and economic circumstances are worlds apart. Schools on the edge face a constant struggle to forge a closer alignment between home and school, parents and teachers, and between the formal world of school and the informal world of neighbourhood and peer group.

Children and young people live nested lives, writes Berliner (2005) referring to the contextual layers of experience through which they attempt to make sense of their world. Failure to grasp the complexity is a weakness of policy that looks for simple remedies, he suggests. So when classrooms do not function as we want them to, we set about improving them. Since those classrooms in turn are in schools, when we decide that those schools are not performing appropriately, we commence 'improving' them as well. But those young people are also situated in families, in neighbourhoods and in peer groups which shape their attitudes and aspirations, often more powerfully than their parents or teachers.

This is a story that could be told in Sydney, Hong Kong, Paris or New York. Politicians and policy-makers often pursue a school improvement path without a textured understanding of what it means for schools to meet the needs of young people on the edge of the social mainstream. These schools serve families and communities that have been cut adrift. The decline of traditional industries in the

NCS	New Community School
NCSL	National College for School Leadership
NFER	National Foundation for Educational Research
NRwS	New Relationship with Schools
OECD	Organisation for Economic Co-operation and Development
Ofsted	Office for Standards in Education
OSHL	Out-of-school Hours Learning
PISA	Programme for International Student Assessment
PLASC	Pupil Level Annual Schools Census
QCA	Qualifications and Curriculum Authority
RML	Ruth Miskin Literacy
SATs	Standard Assessment Tasks
SEN	Special Educational Needs
SFCC	Schools Facing Challenging Circumstances
SFECC	Schools Facing Extremely Challenging Circumstances
SIG	School Improvement Group
SLT	Senior Leadership Team
SMT	Senior Management Team
SRB	Single Regeneration Budget
SSAT	Specialist Schools and Academies Trust
SST	Specialist Schools Trust
UNESCO	United Nations Educational Scientific and Cultural Organization
VAK	Visual, auditory or kinaesthetic

List of Abbreviations

AOTs	Adults other than Teachers
BECTA	British Educational Communications and Technology Agency
CAT	Cognitive Aptitude Test
CPD	Continuing Professional Development
DfES	Department for Education and Skills
EAL	English as an Additional language
EAZ	Educational Action Zone
EBD	Emotional and Behavioural Disorder
EiC	Excellence in Cities Programme
FSM	Free School Meals
GCSE	General Certificate of Secondary Education
GNVQ	General National Vocational Qualification
GTC	General Teaching Council
HMI	Her Majesty's Inspectors
HRO	High Reliability Organisations
HRS	High Reliability School Programme
ICT	Information Communication Technology
INSET	In-Service Education and Training
IQEA	Improving the Quality of Education for All
JARs	Joint Area Reviews
KS2	Key Stage Two
KS3	Key Stage Three
LEA	Local Education Authority
MI	Multiple Intelligences
NAO	National Audit Office

Contents

About the Authors

Jane Cullen is a Research Associate with the Centre for Educational Research and Development (CERD) at the Von Hügel Institute, St Edmund's College Cambridge, and works concurrently with the Open University, East of England. Her research interests are in education in contexts of disadvantage, in widening participation in education, and in discourses in education. She was project manager of the DfES funded evaluation of 'Schools Facing Exceptionally Challenging Circumstances' project. Her current research focuses on regional initiatives to widen participation to higher education. She has come into research from a background of teaching and school management in Asia, South America and Africa.

David Frost is a member of the Educational Leadership and School Improvement team in the Faculty of Education and one of the founder of members of 'Leadership for Learning: the Cambridge Network'. For many years he has worked with teachers, schools and local education authorities to provide frameworks of support for school improvement. His research focuses on 'leadership for learning' with a particular emphasis on teacher leadership. Through partnerships with schools and local authorities he has developed strategies for supporting teachers as agents of change and key actors in the creation and transfer of professional knowledge. He is the founding editor of the journal *Teacher Leadership*.

John Gray is Professor of Education at the University of Cambridge. He has undertaken a number of major studies of school improvement and played a leading role in developing more sophisticated approaches to the evaluation of school performance. He has directed over 60 externally-funded research projects for a wide range of organisations including the ESRC, charities and governmental organisations. He was elected a Fellow of the British Academy in 2000.

John MacBeath is Professor of Educational Leadership at the University of Cambridge. He has written widely on leadership, school improvement and school self-evaluation, his books now translated into twelve languages. He has held a number of consultancies with the OECD, UNESCO, the European Commission, the Hong Kong Government and National Union of Teachers with whom he continues to work closely. He was a member of the Government Task Force on Standards for four years and continues to advise the Executive in his native Scotland. He was awarded the OBE in 1997 for services to education.

Susan Steward worked as a Research Associate in the Faculty of Education from 2001 to 2006. She worked on a number of projects including the 'Inclusion Enigma' sponsored by the National Union of Teachers and the evaluation of the SFECC project on which 'Schools on the Edge' is based.

Sue Swaffield's teaching and research interests are within the fields of educational leadership, school improvement and assessment. Leadership for learning, critical friendship for headteachers, assessment for learning are particular interests. Along with the evaluation of the 'Schools Facing Exceptionally Challenging Circumstances' project, other recent research projects include the ESRC/TLRP 'Learning How to Learn' project, and co-directing the international 'Leadership for Learning Carpe Vitam' project. Sue's work at the University of Cambridge builds on her previous experience as a teacher and adviser.

Acknowledgements

The authors are indebted to the headteachers and staff of the Octet schools for their forbearance and patient co-operation in providing the research team with access to their schools. We appreciate the extent to which they have opened up their practice to scrutiny while continuing to face extremely challenging circumstances on a daily basis.

We are grateful also to the DfES for funding the project on which this book is based, in particular to Sue James who co-ordinated, on its behalf, the Octet intervention that was the subject of our evaluation.

We also acknowledge the essential part played by Helen Cunningham and Dave Ebbutt who worked with the authors as members of the research team.

Thanks are also due to Sally Roach and Janet Gibson of the administrative staff at the University of Cambridge Faculty of Education for their invaluable support.

And to Jude Bowen and Katie Metzler who managed the process from conception to publication.

Paul Chapman Publishing
A SAGE Publications Company
1 Oliver's Yard
55 City Road
London EC1Y 1SP

SAGE Publications Inc
2455 Teller Road
Thousand Oaks, California 91320

SAGE Publications India Pvt Ltd
B-42, Panchsheel Enclave
Post Box 4109
New Delhi 110 017

Library of Congress Control Number: 2006931454

A catalogue record for this book is available from the
British Library

ISBN-10 1-4129-2970-9   ISBN-13 978-1-4129-2970-7
ISBN-10 1-4129-2971-7   ISBN-13 978-1-4129-2971-4 (pbk)

Typeset by C&M Digitals (P) Ltd., Chennai, India
Printed in Great Britain by the Cromwell Press, Trowbridge, Wiltshire
Printed on paper from sustainable resources

Schools on the Edge

Responding to Challenging Circumstances

John MacBeath, John Gray, Jane Cullen, David Frost, Susan Steward and Sue Swaffield

P·CP

Paul Chapman
Publishing

agencies and in relation to offices of government, as children and young people live out their lives in different sites and in often rapid and discontinuous transition from one site to another. The implication for schools is that they become more accountable, not simply for what happens in classrooms or even within schools but in the initiatives they take to liaise and collaborate with other child and family services.

Four decades ago the landmark study in the United States – *Equality of Educational Opportunity* (Coleman et al., 1966) – concluded that it was unreasonable to expect schools to equalise achievement given the unequal distribution of wealth, family 'capital' and privileged access to knowledge and accreditation. A few years later Basil Bernstein (1970) was to write that 'education cannot compensate for society', primarily a reference to schools rather to education more widely conceived.

It was a time of considerable debate as to the place of school in society, the extreme view represented by John Holt's 1970 polemic 'Schools are bad places for children' ([1970] 2005). This theme was taken up by numerous other critics of a school system that was seen as doing disservice to the learning and life chances of children, particularly African-American children (Kozol, 1967). It was also a theme that was to resonate in many countries of the world. In South America Paolo Freire wrote about a 'pedagogy of the oppressed' (1970). In Italy a group of school children wrote a Letter to a Teacher (School of Barbiana, 1969), describing school as a 'hospital that tends to the healthy and neglects the sick'. In Scotland Gow and McPherson (1980) reported, in the words of young people themselves, as 'flung aside' and 'forgotten'. In Sweden Torsten Husen, in Germany Hartman Van Hentig, and in England, Ian Lister called for radical alternatives to the traditional one-size-doesn't-fit-all school.

It is not coincidental that in this climate an alternative stream of research emerged to challenge the prevailing pessimism and bleak narratives of 'compulsory miseducation' (Goodman, 1964). The thesis required an antithesis, and it set in train a search for the counter perspective to offer empirical evidence which might confirm what was known intuitively and anecdotally: that schools could be better places for children and that in the right conditions a school could make a difference to their lives and learning. The search for what came to be known as 'the school effect' did not start from the premise that schools were either intrinsically 'bad' or 'good' for children but that some schools were likely to be better than others at meeting a spectrum of needs and social backgrounds.

What is it about schools that 'makes a difference'?

This is not the place to review the large and complex body of knowledge on school effectiveness which has emerged over the last three decades, but a few key ideas

Every Child Matters?

This opening chapter examines, from the standpoint of children and young people, the extent to which schools have been able to create opportunities for all to succeed. It discusses:

- school and classroom environments which have historically denied opportunities for all children to succeed;
- attempts by school effectiveness and improvement researchers to uncover the secrets of more successful schools;
- the applicability, potential and the limitations of effectiveness/ improvement findings to schools in exceptionally challenging social contexts;
- a curriculum for all, or only for some?

In British education we have long believed that every child matters, yet a naive visitor to our school system might well conclude that some children matter more than others. That the publication of *Every Child Matters* (DfES, 2004a) follows closely, in rhetoric at least, the *No Child Left Behind* US legislation (2001), is not simply coincidental but an expression of concern over the persistent gap between high and low achievers in our respective school systems. Tackling that disparity has been cast by politicians and policy makers as the responsibility of individual schools, an uncompromising message that has often had a demoralising effect on teachers, for whom social and economic odds are seen as too heavily stacked against them.

Every Child Matters is an explicit acknowledgment that schools cannot meet the needs of all children. The subtitle of the document *Change for Children* signals the need for a new relationship, between schools and other community progress the bar was moving inexorably higher as the pressure to perform (and, crucially, be seen to be performing) took hold across the country.

In England, schools perpetually on the margins of national standards, are now described as 'in challenging circumstances'. Within that substantial group of schools the DfES defined an even more disadvantaged sub-set which they termed 'schools facing *exceptionally* challenging circumstances' and which they deemed to be fertile ground for demonstrating that even in the most adverse conditions schools could make dramatic improvement.

Eight schools, selected and recruited by the DfES as a test-bed for examining improvement, are the subject of the second half of this book. They are the prism through which we are enabled to see the larger picture. Through their experiences we come to a more fine grained understanding of how change works, both generally and in varying contexts. These eight schools are unique in their own cultural settings and their developmental history, yet recognisable virtually anywhere in terms of the issues they face. In common with schools in many other places they find themselves trapped in the force field of turbulent communities and uncompromising government policy.

It is the tension between these two sets of pressures that forms the central theme of this book. The first three chapters examine life in communities on the edge and the educational polices intended to provide educational opportunity. The fourth chapter describes the eight schools which signed up for the project designed to show how schools could rise above their circumstances and prevail against the odds, in exchange for the promise of realistic levels of resourcing and support. The stories of this 'Octet' of schools before the intervention of the project are told in this chapter.

The stories as related in Chapter 4 and the evaluation of the SFECC intervention as recounted in the chapters which follow are drawn from an in-depth evaluation study conducted by Cambridge University between 2001 and 2005. The team analysed student performance data over that period, comparing the improvement trajectory of the eight schools with a comparison group, visiting the schools on a regular basis, observing in classrooms, conducting interviews with staff, students and headteachers and, wherever possible, with social/community workers to get an external perspective on these schools (a fuller description of the evaluation project is provided in the Appendix).

Chapter 5 examines the impact on schools of the various initiatives of the SFECC project and evaluates their relative successes and failures. Their success, as measured by attainment at GCSE (the government benchmark for improvement), is the theme of Chapter 6. It analyses student attainment over time and in relation to a set of comparable schools. In light of the findings of the evaluation, the final chapter looks forward to a different kind of future for these schools and all schools which find themselves on the edge.

A matter of attainment

The last decade has witnessed increasing use of so-called 'league tables' to locate school performance. Exam performance has become crucial and schools which are judged not to be up to the mark are deemed suitable cases for treatment. But what counts as 'low attainment' and how many secondary schools might be implicated? Such questions are more difficult to answer.

A report from the National Audit Office (NAO) on 'poorly performing' schools (2006, Figure 14: 23) suggests that in 2001 just over 600 secondary schools had 30 per cent or fewer of their pupils getting five GCSEs at grades A*–C. Judged against national averages, where half the pupils were getting over the same hurdle, all these schools could be described as 'low attaining'. In that year, however, the view of the Department for Education and Skills (DfES) was that 20% represented the minimum acceptable target for all schools. Of the 600 schools just under 200 had less than 20% of their pupils getting over the same hurdle (2006, Figure 14: 23). Only 10% of the schools falling below the 20% hurdle were, according to the NAO's analysis, judged by the Office for Standards in Education (Ofsted) to be 'good' although it does not report what proportion were performing 'satisfactorily' (NAO, 2006: 3).

Defining what might be meant by a 'poorly performing' school is not, however, that straightforward. The same analysis by the National Audit Office (2006, Table 10: 20) suggests that there were a number of different categories of 'poorly performing' schools, all of which might be said to present problems. Three categories were defined by Ofsted's procedures and accounted for some 140 secondary schools. They included: schools in Special Measures which were 'failing to provide an acceptable standard of education' (90 schools); schools with 'serious weaknesses' which were of 'inadequate overall effectiveness' (45); and so-called 'under-achieving' schools which 'performed significantly less well than others in similar contexts' (11). These are schools which might be said to be officially 'under-performing'. However, the DfES also defines schools as 'low attaining' if they are 'failing to achieve adequate levels of attainment for their pupils as measured by GCSE results' (53 schools).

In short, it is difficult to establish precisely how many schools were 'poorly performing' in England in 2001. The Ofsted and DfES categories suggest somewhere between 200 and 300 schools might be in the frame. Whatever the case, for a variety of reasons, the totals were to be reduced considerably over the next three years. The numbers of schools in Special Measures and Serious Weaknesses declined and more schools achieved the earlier 'floor' targets. In 2004 the number of secondary schools not reaching the 30% hurdle was reduced to somewhere over 300 and only around 70 fell below the 20% figure. But whilst such schools were making some from that stream of studies provide a historical and contemporary context for viewing the claim that every child matters and that schools are not necessarily bad places for children. There are at least three ways in which these studies have made a contribution: in terms of the size of the school effect, in respect of factors which may have contributed to it, and the scope for change and improvement.

The evidence is now quite clear that the school a child or young person attends makes a difference to their subsequent progress through the educational system. By the time two pupils 'similar' in terms of their prior attainments reach the secondary stage, the one who is fortunate enough to attend a 'more effective' school is likely to end up with two more GCSE grade C passes than his or her counterpart who attends a 'less effective' school (Gray and Wilcox, 1995: 117).

Of course all pupils make progress as they get older. Research on school effectiveness has been concerned to examine how far such progress is affected by schooling and to answer the question 'What, in particular, are the effects of attending one school as opposed to another?' The two GCSEs estimate is based on comparing the performance of the average pupil attending a school in the top 20% of 'effectiveness' (those which boost pupil progress the most) with the performance of the average pupil attending the bottom 20% (which boost pupil progress the least). A minority of schools and pupils may make more or less progress than this estimate indicates (Gray and Wilcox, 1995: 117). Obtaining two more grade C passes at GCSE than would otherwise have been predicted is not sufficient to transform pupils' life-chances. However, given that the later stages of compulsory and post-compulsory education involve a series of crucial decisions about staying on or leaving, which are undoubtedly influenced by academic performance, its impact at the margins could be considerable – certainly enough to swing a decision one way or the other in determining the fate of any individual pupil.

A major contribution of this research has been to identify some of the factors which have contributed to schools' 'effectiveness' (for a fuller review see Teddlie and Reynolds, 2000). Some common features characterise most of the lists which have been generated. They usually attribute particular significance to the quality of a school's leadership. School culture and ethos are often mentioned along with the importance of high expectations. And the processes of teaching and learning are frequently touched on, along with relationships between schools and their communities (MacBeath and Mortimore, 2001). Policy-makers, in turn, have been enjoined not merely to note the findings but to act upon them.

Given the volume of this research, it is easy to fall into the trap of supposing that there is a consensus about what makes a difference to schools' performance. There has been a tension, however, within the research community, the origins of which go back to the original studies. To many people's surprise the most powerful finding to emerge from Coleman et al.'s pioneering work for the *Equality of Educational Opportunity* survey (1966) was related to a school's 'social mix';

indeed, this turned out to be considerably more important than the levels of teacher experience or resourcing. It was a finding which Rutter et al.'s research was later to echo. 'The academic balance in the intakes to schools was particularly important', he reported. 'Exam success tended to be better in schools with a substantial nucleus of children of at least average intellectual ability' (1979: 178). In other words what really mattered was *who* you went to school with, a case that Thrupp (1999) has made still more forcibly arguing that the main priority for policy-makers should be to seek to influence schools' intakes, an altogether different agenda.

There is a further difficulty for those seeking to use the research to provide pointers to action. Most research on school effectiveness tells us about the pattern of relationships prevailing in a school at the time it was studied. It doesn't necessarily tell us how the school got to be as it is (Gray et al., 1996). Consider, for a moment, the claimed relationship between a school's 'leadership' and its performance. The usual assumption is that a strong head has caused a school to do well and that, conversely, a weak head has caused it to do badly. In truth, however, most research fails to disentangle the causal influences. Strong heads can lead 'good' schools but they can also find themselves in 'bad' ones where, for a variety of reasons, their efforts are frustrated. The new 'tougher' DfES criteria for failing schools set out in the Ofsted website and in its 2005 framework of inspection, gives the following warning to ineffective leadership:

> *Schools require special measures because they are failing to give learners an acceptable standard of education, and when the persons responsible for leading, managing or governing the school are not demonstrating the capacity to secure the necessary improvement. (2005: 17)*

It is easy to understand why a common diagnosis for a school in trouble is that it needs a change of leadership. However, it demands an act of faith to assume that this is the key factor. Changing the leadership may boost the probability of improvement but it is rarely sufficient to guarantee it unless accompanied by many others significant changes.

Research on school improvement

In reality, school *improvement* as a field of research has turned out to be a much messier area than suggested by the initial, and perhaps overly optimistic, forays into school effectiveness. Using knowledge to change things also provides a much stiffer test of what is really known, and the context within which innovation and knowledge are implemented assumes crucial importance.

Earlier research on secondary schools identified three different ways in which schools tackle their improvement agendas; these were called 'tactical', 'strategic' and 'capacity-building' (see Gray et al., 1999). Almost all schools have adopted so-called 'tactical' approaches at one time or another. They focus their efforts, for example, on trying to raise the results of pupils who are predicted to get grades D to grades C and enter some pupils for more exams. Teachers and pupils alike are enjoined to 'work harder' and, for a while, many do. The weakness of this approach, of course, is that after varying (but mostly relatively short) periods of time the initial impetus begins to fade.

Schools which adopt 'strategic' approaches to improvement have tended to enjoy more success. They often have a well-developed analysis of what they need to do and tackle the resulting agenda in a fairly systematic way. They may undertake an in-depth review of the issues in a particular department or launch a school-wide initiative. What distinguishes them from other schools, however, is the measured way in which they take up their challenges.

'Capacity-building' schools go still further by finding ways to involve the majority of their staff not only in setting the improvement agenda but also in its active implementation. What particularly characterises these schools is their continuing determination to focus improvement efforts on issues arising directly from the quality of teaching and learning.

Most schools develop 'tactical' approaches to improvement; unfortunately, in many schools, this is the dominant way in which they tend to tackle change. Some schools succeed in being 'strategic' most of the time and some others manage it some of the time. But very few schools, in the judgment of the research team, reach the 'capacity-building' stage. The challenge for schools seems to lie in recognising how they routinely tackle change issues and in seeking, over time, to develop and (where necessary) rebuild some of the ways in which they do so. The more issues related to aspects of learning and teaching that can be brought into focus, the better the prognosis is likely to be.

School improvers tend to attribute considerable importance to creating collaborative partnerships in which all the partners (heads, teachers, almost certainly pupils and, in some accounts, local communities) realise that they can benefit from reform and commit themselves to it. Whilst it is often assumed in such accounts that the headteacher will both supply and sustain the vision, it is usually recognised that if others are to implement it, they need to 'own' it too – they need to feel they have participated in its planning and construction.

Familiar patterns of leadership in the school may need challenging and even reconstruction. Heads and senior leaders, for their part, are enjoined to adopt leadership styles which are transformational and to commit themselves to patterns of distributed leadership in which a larger group of professionals have a stake. To effect such change and enhance the leadership capabilities of a school may require the support of an external consultant or adviser. At the same time teachers are expected to develop new skills and to commit themselves to professional development activities, preferably working directly on their school's agenda. The hope is that the energies thereby released will address themselves to the school's most pressing problems which are likely to be found in the processes of classroom teaching and learning themselves (Stoll et al., 2003). Over time and through these means, the school's 'capacity for change' should be enhanced.

There is another side to school improvement, nonetheless, which this essentially optimistic account ignores at its peril. Both pressure *and* support, Fullan (2000) has argued, are necessary for change to take place. It is a telling phrase, capturing the two sides of the change equation. Pressure can come from many sources, most fruitfully perhaps from within the school itself or from a 'critical friend' (Swaffield and MacBeath, 2005). However, in a climate of increasing accountability, schools have found themselves having to cope with the judgments of others as expressed through league tables, Ofsted reports and parental choice. Faced with such pressures, taking the 'long view' may not always seem like an option.

How long can schools maintain an upward trajectory? The evidence suggests that school improvement seems to come in bursts. Changes to aspects of practice and provision may be a continuing process that continues over a number of years. But, in most schools, three years seems to represent an upper limit as far as improving measured results is concerned (Mangan et al., 2005). Improvement then seems to tail off. Over a ten year period Thomas et al. (in press) found that only a minority of schools, perhaps up to 40%, might be able to deliver a second burst. For the majority of schools, then, building capacity and *sustaining* improvement over time seems to pose a formidable challenge.

The research on school improvement provides some useful starting points but there is a further problem for practitioners and policy-makers concerned to tackle performance levels in particularly disadvantaged areas. Much of the existing evidence is drawn from contexts where the conditions for change were probably more favourable.

A seamless web of circumstance

In the 1960s the Plowden Committee (1967) drew attention to the challenges facing the educational system in dealing with the problems of social disadvantage. Disadvantaged children, they argued, were trapped by their backgrounds and by their schools in 'a seamless web of circumstance'. Thirty years on the National Commission on Education provided a similar analysis. 'In deprived areas', they wrote, 'multiple disadvantages combine to make educational success difficult to attain' (1995: 7).

Interestingly, both bodies provided similar prescriptions. Plowden argued that the first step must be to bring the schools the poor attended up to national standards; the second 'quite deliberately' to make them better (1967). However, the sustained attack on the causes of under-performance associated with social disadvantage which Plowden called for did not take place on the scale envisaged. Indeed, the National Commission's warning echoed Plowden's: 'the fact is the dice are loaded against any school in such areas'. They acknowledged that there were 'many schools which do well in discouraging circumstances' but the 'odds were stacked against them' (1996: 5).

The case studies of schools succeeding 'against the odds', commissioned by the National Commission on Education (1996), with a follow-up study of the same schools five years later (Maden, 2001), provide two exceptions to an otherwise depressing picture. How far can schools break free of the constraints imposed by society? The evidence certainly suggests that a small minority seem to. Do their experiences offer broader lessons and cause for optimism? Some would argue that they do. But before we embrace this position we need to remind ourselves of the scale of the challenge.

The enduring nature of inequality

Since Coleman's landmark report four decades ago it might be argued that for those 'flung aside forgotten children' (Gow and McPherson, 1980) much has changed or, alternatively that little has changed, depending on the lens through which it is viewed. In England, at the time the Coleman team wrote their report, grammar schools were alive and well and admitting something between 10% and 20% of primary children on the basis of tests of their 'potential' at the age of eleven. This winnowing out of children on the verge of puberty provided an 'efficient' sifting mechanism but caused the Robbins Commission in 1963 to express concern over the 'pool of untapped talent'. At that time 11% of young people sat A level exams, a figure that was to quadruple within three decades. From around 4% being admitted to university in the early Sixties the percentage is now approaching 50%. 'The limited pool has been transformed into a copious flood' wrote Coffield and Vignoles (1998: Report 5), taking issue with the conclusion of the Dearing Committee who had, in 1997, predicted that the 'ceiling of academically-minded young people' had been reached (DfES, 1997: 5).

The scale of such changes within our lifetimes challenges limiting notions of 'ability' and 'potential', and opens to question the organisational structures which both channel and constrain opportunities to learn. They tell us that school can be an obstacle as well as a pathway to higher levels of learning and economic and social welfare. But there are also counter trends. Policy development is not always about reducing inequalities, as when these data are viewed through a darker lens a continuing gap between the most and least privileged is revealed. An examination of university access by social class (Vignoles et al., 2004) concluded that inequality was much the same as two decades earlier, although it did reveal that for a time in the 1990s the social class gap was actually widening. While there were now more young people from working class backgrounds in higher education, the differential between them and their middle class peers had not diminished (72–3). From 1994–95 to 2001–02 the proportion of young people from families in areas with average annual incomes of below £10,950 rose from 0.89% to 1.77% while in areas with an average income of £21,890 the rate of increase was from 10.04% to 19.16%. (National Statistics, 2005).

Differential achievement at school and access to higher education have remained closely correlated to social background and income. As the Institute for Fiscal Studies (Brewer et al., 2005) reports, inequality in original income (before taking account of taxes and benefits) increased steadily throughout the 1980s and has remained relatively stable since then. The top fifth is still about four times better off than the bottom fifth of the population (National Statistics, 2005). Explanations for this higher level of inequality since the start of the 1980s include:

- an increase in the gap between wages for skilled and unskilled workers which is in part due to skills-biased technological change and a decline in the role of trade unions;
- growth in self-employment income and in unemployment;
- a decrease in the rate of male participation in the labour market, often in households where there is no other earner; and
- increased female participation among those with working partners, leading to an increased polarisation between two-earner and zero-earner households.

Despite improved access to formal education for more young people, initiatives to close the gap have continued to be frustrated by factors lying largely outside schools. The Mental Health Foundation estimates that 15% of pre-school children have 'mild' mental health problems, and 7% have problems described as 'severe' (Mental Health Foundation, 2005). These rates fall disproportionately on disadvantaged neighbourhoods, with the highest rates of mental disorders occurring among children from families where no parent has ever worked. The World Health Organisation (2005) estimates that 8% of all girls and 2% of all boys in the country show symptoms of severe depression. In the 5–10 age group, 10% of boys and 6% of girls are affected, and among the 11–15 age group, 13% of boys and 10% of girls. There is also a clear link between mental disorders and rates of smoking, alcohol consumption and cannabis use, most prevalent in the most economically deprived areas. People from the poorest areas in the country are nearly three times as likely to be admitted to hospital for depression as those who are not, and are three times more likely to commit suicide. One out of four of these young people who take their own lives will have been in contact with mental health services in the previous year. Poorer people are also six times more likely to be admitted to hospital with schizophrenia, and ten times more likely to be admitted for alcohol-related problems. Between 10% and 20% of young people involved in criminal activity are thought to have a psychiatric disorder.

Education counts

While such factors impact powerfully on young people's engagement with schooling, there is data to show that schools can make a difference to psychological health. For example, ESRC data (Society Today Fact Sheet, 2005) suggests that, even for children from the least privileged social backgrounds, gaining educational qualifications and experiencing good adjustment in childhood contribute to protecting individuals from psychological problems in adulthood. Schools can provide an oasis of order and safety and a temporary escape from the turbulence of the world beyond their gates. The bulk of evidence tells us, however, that they can rarely do it alone.

If *every* child matters, then there has to be more than the temporary relief offered by 15,000 hours spent in the classroom. If every child is to have a genuine opportunity to gain qualifications and meet the five DfES 'outcomes' (staying healthy, enjoying and achieving, keeping safe, contributing to the community, and social and economic well-being), there has be not only a concerted provision of services to children and families but a more imaginative response to the multiplicity of disadvantages faced by young people and their families (DfES, 2004a)

In recognition of this many local authorities are now moving towards child and family services. The Hertfordshire local authority was the first in the country to move from segmented administrative divisions (or SILOS), in which the Education service maintained a largely independent existence, to more broadly encompassing Children and Family Services. Ray Shostak, Hertfordshire's then Director of Education, illustrated the need for more joined-up services by citing the case of Carole and her family, as depicted in Figure 1.1 This may be an extreme case but the graphic depiction makes the point about the minefield that some parents have to negotiate in order to access the services that meet a range of complex physical, psychological and health needs.

Children like Carole, caught in a web of circumstance not of their own making, rely on parents or other carers who have the skills to successfully negotiate their way through the thickets of welfare and educational agencies. For parents in communities on the edge this means juggling child minding, employment, and domestic upkeep including guarding vulnerable property against ever present threats from a new generation of lawlessness. For children and young people success is equally a matter of navigation. Success in school is not simply a matter of academic ability but the ability to understand and 'play the system', reliant on motivation, commitment and perseverance in the face of failure – a legacy for young people that may not be within the family inheritance. As we know from

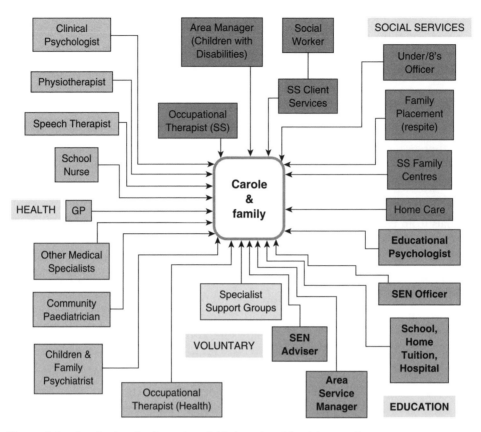

Figure 1.1   Carole, her family and social/educational/health agencies
Source: Presentation by Ray Shostak, Director of Children and Family Services.

numerous studies (Jencks et al., 1972; Weiss and Fine, 2000; Epstein, 2004), parental length of time in formal education is mirrored by the next generation. Parental interest in their children's future is likely to be even more crucial: as Feinstein and Symons (1999: 301) observe, out of the effects of parental, peer group and schooling inputs, the most powerful is 'parental interest'.

Exploring the links between levels of numeracy and home, school and community an Australian government study (University of Queensland, 2004) identified key factors that inhibited and promoted success for children. One of the major obstacles was the lack of knowledge among school staff about resources for learning that lay outside the school, for example in playgroups, after-school care or other informal contexts. Trying to raise standards within the school alone was an unequal struggle without bridges into other learning sites. Success was more likely when there was:

- already a history of relationship-building between home and school;
- a specific focus on local needs;

- leadership and liaison by one or two 'champions' (powerful advocates);
- continuity of provision of financial, material and human resources;
- appropriate professional development for teachers; and
- a horizontal structure that often featured cross-sectoral or multi-agency networks or community-based agencies.

These findings are paralleled by a long tradition of research in the UK (MacBeath et al., 1986; Bastiani, 1987; Wolfendale, 1992). Much of this literature reveals the hiatus between home and school, the inhibitions around what a school would describe as 'parental involvement' and what a parent might describe as 'teacher involvement'. From a parental viewpoint there has been an investment in a child's learning for five critical years before he or she passes the child into the school's care, yet when parents and teachers meet in the context of parent evenings, there is an asymmetry in the power balance, especially for parents whose school life had proved an unrewarding or even alienating experience. It is an occasion, as Nalaskowski (quoted in Mendel, 2003: 7) describes as, 'saturated with immaturity', the small classroom desks all too redolent of frustration and inadequacy. Lawrence-Lightfoot describes the parent–teacher meeting as marked by decorum and politeness, wariness and defensive postures, infused with histories on both sides of the table in which 'meta-messages remain hidden, inaudible, unarticulated. They are the raw, unvarnished subtext to the ritualized, polite, public text of the conversation' (2003: 33).

Coping with teachers is only part of the challenge. It is not hard to imagine that Carole, symbolic of children lost in the institutional nexus, might have ended her life as tragically as Victoria Climbié, the seven-year-old girl who was to provide the catalyst and impetus for the Children Act of 2004. Victoria was subjected to systematic abuse by her carers and forced to sleep in the bath tied up inside a black plastic sack, leading eventually to her death. Following Victoria's death an inquiry led by Lord Laming (2003) provided damning reading, describing the case as a catalogue of administrative, managerial and professional failure by the services responsible for the welfare of children. Over a nine month period between 1999 and 2000 Victoria was known to four social services departments, three housing departments and two specialist child protection teams of the Metropolitan Police. She was admitted to two different hospitals because of concerns that she was being deliberately harmed and was referred to a specialist Children and Families centre managed by the National Society for the Protection of Children (NSPCC). In Brent, one local authority, says Lord Laming, gave 'Victoria's case ... no fewer than five "unique" reference numbers. Retrieving files, I was told, was like the national lottery, and with similar odds' (Victoria Climbié Inquiry, 2003, Speech by Lord Laming, 2003).

It is in the most disadvantaged of schools and classrooms that Caroles and Victorias are most likely to be found, perhaps invisible or perhaps 'difficult', perhaps erratic in attendance and emotional response, or even compliant and on the surface apparently happy. As Carole and Victoria are extreme cases it may be more helpful to view the challenges of school through the experience of a more middle of the road young person, brought up by caring parents, concerned for his education but struggling to survive against-the-odds. Although Jonathan and his mother live on the White City housing estate in London, it could just as easily be in Benwell in Newcastle, Moss Side in Manchester or Scotland Street in Liverpool. Jonathan, whose anonymised story comes from interviews conducted with community workers and young people in Hammersmith and Fulham, is chosen as a 'typical' rather than an extreme example.

CASE STUDY

Jonathan

Jonathan, fourteen and a half, lives in a council flat with his mother and three younger brothers. His father was keen for Jonathan to do well and although he worked long hours he generally found time to talk to his children about their school work. Since Jonathan's father's death, his mother has found it difficult to manage the family on benefits and has a part-time job, depending on Jonathan to help in the home and look after his three siblings. Although Jonathan likes school he has to stay at home when his mother is ill or has to work unsocial hours, so his attendance is erratic and he is often late into school in the morning. Having given up on homework, partly due to lack of time, space and domestic chores, he is getting into more and more trouble at school. Constant latecoming and failing to turn up for detention have made him less inclined to want to go to school and he has skipped periods on days when he has science or maths because he says those teachers 'give all their attention to the white kids'. He is able to intercept letters home so his mother never receives invitations to attend parent evenings or expressions of concern about his behaviour. His occasional truanting has brought him into contact with other young people excluded from school, and he has been initiated into some of the skills of shoplifting. The more he sees of the world outside school, the less meaningful he finds what he is being taught in school.

The challenge for schooling

The obstacles to success which Jonathan would have to surmount to succeed academically may be seen as, on the one hand, external to the school but, on the other, internal to the structure and modus operandi of the school itself. It is, in fact, the interplay of these two sets of conditions which needs to be understood if obstacles are to be removed and opportunities created. Where the school fails to connect with Jonathan's experience, or with the thousands of young people like him, may be described in terms of structures, relationships, curriculum relevance and assessment, incentives and sanctions.

The inflexible structure of the school day does not easily mesh with patterns of home life. Many young people, very often girls, shoulder responsibilities for their younger siblings and sometimes for parents who might be ill, disabled or simply not up to the multiple demands of child care and education. From the school's perspective it is difficult to allow exceptions or to know what might be justifiable reasons for lateness or absence, having no immediate links into the home environment except at second-hand through social or community workers. The nature of the timetabled day allows for selective attendance at certain periods but also penalises students who miss out. With little chance to catch up, they fall progressively further behind due to the relentless pace over the ground to be covered. The periodic structure of the school day, with its consecutive slices of subjects requiring successive shifts of focus and expectations, is widely accepted as an unsatisfactory way to organise learning yet has proved intractable due to an interlocking set of factors which conspire to defeat more radical alternatives. As attendance is used as a public indicator of a school's quality, the pressure is on the school to use whatever measures might be deemed to work to get students through the door and to try to accommodate learning and teaching within a set of given structures.

We read commonly in policy documents about helping children to 'access the curriculum' and, within this paradigm, equity is tested by the efforts schools and teachers make to reduce what is often a gap in attainment between children at one level, grade or key stage and their peers. This is brought home most sharply in respect of children with 'special needs', whose teachers struggle vainly to engage them with arcane topics far removed from their interests in both senses of that word. But it is not only that group of children so categorised for whom the curriculum is not a vehicle but an impediment to their learning. Eisner (2006) has spoken about the 'null curriculum', referring to what we teach by what we don't pay attention to.

The curriculum comprises a body of knowledge deemed to represent what Matthew Arnold in 1869 described as the 'best that has been thought and said', judged by framers of the National Curriculum to be apposite and applicable to all children no matter their circumstances. It is a model of knowledge premised on a number of essential conditions which, when observed, may be deemed to provide a rounded educational experience. When those conditions are not present, however, it can become a serious obstacle rather than a learning opportunity. Its rhythm, locked into the structure of the school day, is 'ruthlessly cumulative'

(Pinker, 1999: 56); without remedial loops and sustained support it becomes progressively harder for young people to engage or re-engage.

Teachers in a London school, one of eight schools facing exceptionally challenging circumstances, talked about a 'groundhog day', a reference to the film in which Bill Murray wakes every morning to relive the same day over and over again. For some young people and their teachers it seemed as if every lesson was a revisiting of what had gone the day before, as if the slate had been wiped clean overnight. Taking into account the gap between a history lesson on a Friday and the next on a Tuesday, separated by myriad domestic and community competing priorities and tensions, it takes little imagination to perceive the disconnections between in-school and out-of- school learning.

The classroom as a key site for learning

The curriculum is 'delivered' within classrooms. The language of delivery is an apt one to describe the traditional process through which knowledge passes from teacher to students. While much has changed in the last few years to make classroom learning more interactive, more learner focused and more vivid through the use of information and whiteboard technology, the thirty students deskbound structure of the typical classroom hems in opportunities for a more flexible, less time constrained, less episodic exposure to ideas and a less reflective pace of thinking. What happens in the passage of knowledge is caricatured by Hargreaves (2003) as a tube through which knowledge passes from teacher to students but which in fact inhibits its passage by misconception, self belief, lack of prior learning and inappropriate medium, to which might be added preferred learning 'style'.

It is this all too human dimension of learning that renders the seemingly neutral delivery metaphor so inappropriate and illuminates the difference between a curriculum-centred view of the world and a learning-centred view. A learning-centred view works between the learner(s) and what we know about learning and then interrogates the curriculum with a critical eye.

> *More importance is placed on exploration than discovery, more value is assigned to surprise than to control, more attention is devoted to what is distinctive than to what is standard, more interest is related to what is metaphorical than to what is literal. It is an educational culture that has a greater focus on becoming than on being, places more value on the imaginative than on the factual, assigns greater priority to valuing than to measuring, and regards the quality of the journey as more significant than the speed at which the destination is reached.* (Eisner, 2002: 16)

If teaching is genuinely to stimulate learning it requires both a context and a form of communication that is alive to the moment, that is able to connect with the learner's 'bandwidth' (Qvortrup, 2001), a process of fine tuning and continuous retuning as the learner or teacher drift off the selected waveband. The potential for finding and maintaining the bandwidth is dependent on a number of antecedent factors. It presupposes an ability on the part of the teacher to create a social climate for learning with a willingness to risk straying beyond the confines of a curricular and methodological straitjacket.

This is turn assumes a quality of school leadership which is directed to building a culture in which learning is safe, adventurous and significant to the learner. In the United States this is described by the totally inappropriate term 'instructional leadership', now slowly being superseded by the more telling 'learning-focused leadership' (Knapp et al., 2006). This denotes a leadership which pays attention to the diversity of learning needs, not just of pupils but of teachers, of ancillary staff and the needs of the school itself as a community which learns. Seeing others learning, and in particular those high status people – teachers and school leaders – is what makes learning both visible and catching. Perkins puts it this way:

> ... *imagine learning to dance when the dancers around you are all invisible. Imagine learning a sport when the players who already know the game can't be seen ... As educators, we can work to make thinking much more visible than it usually is in classrooms. When we do so, we are giving students more to build on and learn from. By making the dancers visible, we are making it much easier to learn to dance.* (2004: 1)

Learning as a social activity is modelled in a milieu within which we observe and internalise norms in which the learner both 'catches' and 'spreads' ideas. Knowing and remembering occur because knowledge and memory are invested in, and accessible from, the behaviours and intelligences of people with whom we share and create ideas. When the environment is rich in intellectual challenge – whether in the classroom, the home, the peer group or the community – learning thrives and grows, and when there is a synergy across these various 'construction sites' learning is without limits.

QUESTIONS FOR REFLECTION AND DISCUSSION

1. In what ways have school effectiveness and improvement research had an impact on the lives of children in disadvantaged circumstances?

2. In your experience how do the 'improvement' categories of tactical, strategic and capacity-building apply to school and classroom practice?

3. 'Potential' and 'ability' are cited as examples of concepts that limit thinking and constrain practice. What other terminology in current use might be added to the list?
4. In what ways may the 'seamless web of circumstance' be used as a framing idea to explore the relationship between neighbourhood cultures and the culture of the school?
5. How can success be measured for the five 'outcomes' of Every Child Matters?

2

A Matter of Policy

Chapter 1 discussed from a 'worm's eye view' of children and young people the context in which they 'matter' to schools and their often inhibiting conventions. Chapter 2 addresses these issues from the bird's eye view of policy. It examines:

- the continuing nature of the achievement gap;
- the achievements of comprehensive schools, the mounting critique of their efficacy and the search for alternatives;
- the pursuit of diversity in national and local authority policy and in school and classroom practice;
- three specific improvement initiatives and discusses their potential and limitations.

Addressing the achievement gap

For nearly half a century governments around the world have tried to address the conspicuous gap between high and low school achievers. However, as a policy drive this really only began in earnest when researchers and government agencies began to collect data on differential student performance and made the link to the prosperity of the economy and international competitiveness. Orfield has argued that in the United States up until 1966 the government did not gather data by ethnicity because such data would expose sharply unequal outcomes and that 'it would be better off not knowing' (1998: 166). Even today many countries still do not collect such data, considering it too sensitive and an infringement of human rights, or perhaps because they also fear exposure of stark differentials between those young people in the centre and those on the edge.

As researchers and government agencies began to collect data more systematically, wide disparities in achievement surfaced more insistently and policy makers turned their attention to comparative performance of schools. This current of policy development was strengthened considerably by the growing stream of effectiveness studies which, as Chapter 1 showed, suggested that schools are differentially successful in raising standards of student performance, even when social class is taken into account. The evidence on race has been less thoroughly explored but for many (although not all) ethnic groups points to the same conclusions (Gillborn and Mirza, 2000; Gillborn and Youdell, 2000).

Prior to the advent of comprehensive schools, the structural arrangements of a tripartite system in England masked some of the disparities in achievement as grammar, secondary modern and vocational schools were supposedly designed to match ability and potential. As numerous studies were to illustrate (see for example Harlen and Malcolm's 1999 review of research), selective mechanisms proved another variation on the self-fulfilling prophecy, constraining and narrowing the pool of potential talent.

Landmark reports such as Newsom in 1963 documented the wastage of *Half our Future*, as that document was tellingly entitled. It laid some of the groundwork for the move to a comprehensive system in 1965 under the Labour government (circular 10/65) requiring all local education authorities to 'go comprehensive'. The move was in part fuelled by a growing body of evidence on inequities in the system but also in part by pressure from middle class parents dissatisfied with standards in secondary modern schools where many of their children found themselves after the 11 plus. The 10/65 mandate, reversed by Margaret Thatcher as Secretary of State for Education in 1970, allowed authorities choice of future direction, the consequences of which are still felt today. In 2006 nearly a quarter of all local authorities retained selective systems, despite a 1996 declaration by Prime Minister in-waiting, Tony Blair, calling time on selection:

> *The grammar school system ... was a response to the needs of a vanished society which required a small educated class and a large number of manual workers. It is no longer the appropriate model for a world where most jobs require educated men and women.* (October 1996)

Comprehensivisation was a major step to closing the achievement gap and despite decades of criticism, claims and counter claims, the evidence, on balance, suggests that comprehensive schools are somewhat more likely to push up student performance standards than selective systems. For example, a value-added comparison of selective and non-selective local authorities showed that the overall effect of selection was to depress overall performance; while grammar schools did well for the pupils they selected, the performance of the other 75% was lower than in non-selective systems (Jesson, 2000). In fact even comparison of the

top 25% in grammar and comprehensive schools showed little difference with comprehensive school performing marginally better, in spite of the wide disparity in social class intake. In a House of Commons reply in November 2002 the Minister reported that in grammar schools the average percentage of children eligible for free school meals was 2.9% compared with an English average of 17.3% (Parliamentary Answer, 1 November 2002).

Nonetheless, evidence on closing the gap by social class background continues to disappoint those who saw comprehensive schools as equalising outcomes and not just offering equality of opportunity. In the more even playing field in Scotland where 97 per cent of children attend all-through comprehensive schools (with the remaining 3% in the independent sector), there is data to show a closing of the social class gap (Croxford, 2000). Nor, among Scottish policy makers, is there an echo of Ruth Kelly's critique, suggesting that comprehensive schools have served their purpose and that it is time to move on to more varied forms of provision.

Comprehensive schools have raised standards and done well for many pupils, but they do not seem to have been the universal engine of social mobility and equality that Crosland hoped they would be. They played a vital role in overcoming the institutionalised two-tierism that was inherent in selection, but for too many people they have not delivered what he called social equality, what today we call social justice. (Kelly, 2005b)

The search for alternatives

While there has been much opposition to any compromise of the comprehensive ideal, the hope it nourished for a more egalitarian system was not forthcoming and there was a swelling tide of opinion that the needs of disadvantaged children could be better addressed through some forms of specialised and targeted provision. In the US, where comprehensive schools had long been the status quo, there was mounting evidence of school failure to equalise opportunity (Coleman et al., 1966; Jencks, 1972; Kozol, 1991), leading to a mushrooming of alternative schools or centres around the country, many based on A.S. Neill's Summerhill School. These found common cause with the high profile, but short lived, deschooling movement which promulgated 'convivial' alternatives to school. The alternative and deschooling movements had a brief life in both the US and the UK in the 1970s, as the more 'democratic' and innovative approaches were co-opted into mainstream provision attempting to make schools more democratic, less like the traditional egg box school and more open to their local communities, By the mid 1970s there were secondary schools in Scotland with over a hundred adults learning alongside young people in mainstream classrooms.

Numerous reasons may be advanced for the end of radical alternatives: the energy, commitment and financial support needed to keep them going; 'reschooling', focused on improving schools in the mainstream; and the growing influence of the school effectiveness 'movement'. Perhaps, most significantly, a changing political climate initiated by James Callaghan with his 'Great Debate' on education in 1976, the Thatcher–Reagan era of high pressure, high stakes schooling, and a return to 'basics' signalling the death knell of 'progressivism'.

A curriculum for all

Integral to the comprehensive ideal was a common curriculum. Exposure of all children to the same diet from five until fourteen would, it was hoped, prevent early differentiation into academic and non-academic streams. It was argued that a common curriculum would no longer exclude some children from the opportunity to progress to higher education and gain the academic certification demanded by employers. While first mooted in the mid-Seventies under Callaghan's Labour government, it was not until the 1988 Act that a National Curriculum was put in place. It was described by Davies and Evans as 'constructed from a collection of school subjects on the assumption that a coherent whole would emerge from the sum of the parts' (2001: 97). Running in tandem with the drive for curriculum uniformity was the attempt to align the curriculum with the needs of employers and of the economy more generally. However, the tensions and contradictions have been manifest, weakening attempts to create a system able to address the wide spectrum of needs, dispositions, social experiences and family legacies.

From uniformity to diversity

Despite its embrace of a national curriculum, the Conservative government continued to champion diversity in the form of grammar schools, secondary moderns and comprehensives. These continued in many areas of the country to exist side by side, offering a weak form of equality in which schools were seen as matched to individual needs and abilities. While New Labour from 1997 onwards stoutly opposed selection, the 'bog standard'[1] comprehensive school was subject to a slow process of attrition. It was defended by Ministers at the same time as its foundations were being slowly eroded.

> *Ours is a vision of a school system which values opportunity for all, and embraces diversity and autonomy as the means to achieve it. **Autonomy** so that well led schools take full responsibility for their mission. **Diversity** so that schools – individually and as a broader family locally and nationally – cater significantly better for the diverse requirements and aspirations of today's young people.* (emphasis, added)

What this statement makes clear in the two emboldened words is schools as self improving but also with scope to pursue their own path in response to the communities they serve. In her foreword to the White Paper (*Higher Standards, Better Schools for All, 2005a*) Ruth Kelly, then Secretary of State, gave explicit recognition to the achievement gap as located in the social class divide.

> *The attainment gap between high and low achieving schools is too great. And a child's educational achievements are still too strongly linked to their parents' social and economic background, a key barrier to social mobility.* (2005a: 9)

The solution therefore was to be achieved by 'putting parents and the needs of their children at the heart of our school system', a system 'increasingly driven by parents and by choice', with parents having a 'real say' in how schools are run (p. 6).

> *We believe parents should have greater power to drive the new system: it should be easier for them to replace the leadership or set up new schools where they are dissatisfied with existing schools* (p. 6)

These proposals are elaborated further in Chapter 2 of the White Paper entitled 'A School System Shaped by Parents,' and in Chapter 5 'Parents Driving Improvement'. The appointment of someone described as a 'parents' champion' would, it was proposed, 'help parents understand the nature of the problems at their school and the options available to address them' (p. 35). These 'dedicated choice advisers' would help the least well-off parents to exercise their choices which would be facilitated through the right to free school transport to their three nearest secondary schools within a six mile radius.

In this ministerial vision a central role is accorded to performance tables and inspections, seen as an 'important pressure on weaker schools to improve' (p. 5). By these means the government 'sets expectations, provides support and intervenes to tackle failure and under-performance in deprived areas'. At the same time 'Ofsted's sharper inspection regime', it was envisaged, 'will hold schools to account for how every child performs'. How far the logic of such approaches maps directly onto the experiences of disadvantaged communities is, however, doubtful. Both performance tables and inspection are more likely than not to signal to the most informed and ambitious of parents that they should look elsewhere.

Improvement through inspection?

In reality, inspection is a blunter instrument than policy-makers have often assumed. It can help to hold schools to account but its capacity to bring about 'improvement' is more in doubt. Kenneth Baker's visions of 'big cats prowling the educational landscape' (Learmonth, 2000: 33) promised a radical shake up of a system that was perceived to be failing children. However, the recognition that the circumstances under which inspection can 'make a difference' are more circumscribed than previously assumed, has taken more than a decade to emerge. After three successive studies showing no necessary link between schools being inspected and subsequent improvements in their academic performance (Cullingford and Daniels, 1998; Shaw et al., 2003; Rosenthal, 2004), Ofsted itself undertook its own analysis. They found that in some years inspected schools made greater progress than those that were not inspected, in other years they didn't. Ofsted commented that 'there is little significance to be read into this [pattern of results], except to say that inspection is neither a catalyst for instant improvement in GCSE results nor a significant inhibitor' (Matthews and Sammons, 2004: 37).

In short, when and how inspection makes a difference depends on context and circumstance. It is unlikely to be the universal panacea its supporters maintain. It is a fact that schools serving disadvantaged communities are more likely to find themselves more frequently on the wrong end of inspectors' judgments (Gray, 2000). It does not necessarily follow from this that they are more likely to benefit as a result of persisting pressure to improve.

The New Relationship with Schools (NRwS, DfES, 2004b) envisages some recasting of the elements of the accountability procedure. It is presented as a seven piece jigsaw with self-evaluation as the centre piece, monitored more frequently and with shorter and sharper visits by inspectors. As the New Relationship matures it is planned that it will widen its compass to embrace emerging national policies and judge schools not only on the basis of their performance but on the alliances they have forged with other social agencies. The five 'outcomes' of the Every Child Matters agenda (see Chapter 1) will be integral to an emerging accountability system which will, in time, require a very different form of performance tables as the contributions to raising engagement and achievement are diffused among various agencies and take account of learning in and out of school. It is an ambitious agenda but one with which many schools in disadvantaged areas may struggle.

Local authorities: from old to new diversities

From time to time newspapers produce maps of Britain showing wide regional disparities in housing costs, health, life expectancy and other indicators of quality of life. These tend to correlate closely with a mapping of educational achievement, and so-called 'league tables' provide their own map of how class and race play out in school performance. Closing the gap has, since the mid 1960s, implied some form of positive discrimination at area or local authority level.

The idea of Educational Priority Areas was first proposed in the Plowden Report of 1967. Its hope was that by positively discriminating on an area basis it would help to 'break the vicious cycle of deprivation'. It depicted a world of childhood in deprived areas as a 'seamless web of circumstance'.

The world in which the children grow up, [is one] where everything influences everything else, where nothing succeeds like success and nothing fails like failure. The outlook and aspiration of their own parents; the opportunities and handicaps of the neighbourhood in which they live; the skill of their teachers and the resources of the schools they go to; their genetic inheritance; and other factors still unmeasured or unknown surround the children with a seamless web of circumstance. (1967: para 131)

The Report went on to argue for positive discrimination on the grounds of the 'special challenges' for teachers having to deal with the potential conflict of values between home and school and that 'however good the opportunities, some children may not be able to take advantage of them. Failure may have taken away from them their urge to learn' (para 136).

Reviewing the impact of Plowden twenty years on Kogan (1987) argued that it was typical of 'the British way'. The evangelical purpose and optimistic assumption about the ability to cause change by exemplary description has, he suggests, been endemic to the British tradition of advisory committees shaping policy. Kogan sees a deep fault line in the strong endorsement of professional individuality, a position which is difficult to reconcile with the vision of schools working across institutional and professional boundaries. The role of teachers as agents of social change rests, he contends, on an act of faith rather than any realistic assessment of the professional and micro-political territory.

In Scotland, Strathclyde Region's ambitious Social Strategy for the Eighties (followed a decade later by A Social Strategy for the Nineties) made some notable achievements in areas of priority but also highlighted the immense difficulties faced by teachers in working with social workers, police, welfare rights workers, educational psychologists and housing officials. Each of these groups brought widely differing value systems, working practices, professional and political affiliations to their work with children, young people and their families.

The reincarnation of educational priority areas under New Labour as Education Action Zones (EAZs), introduced in England in 1998 and in Northern Ireland in 2003, never succeeded in fulfilling their more radical intent. The 73 zones serving 1,444 schools covering approximately 6% of the school population in England were afforded latitude to be innovative, to ignore the full national curriculum if they wished, to focus on literacy and numeracy, as well as sidestep national agreements on pay and conditions in order to attract the right kind of staff. The finding that EAZs had 'not often been test beds of genuinely innovative action' led, in November 2001 to Zones being amalgamated into the Excellence for Schools initiative (Ofsted, 2001: 1).

The failure of one initiative after another to make a significant impact on the achievement gap only served to step up the government search for the Holy Grail of equality of outcome. The Excellence in Cities (EiC) programme, launched in 1999, was the next attempt to focus on raising standards in urban conurbations where the cumulative effects of disadvantage were most in evidence. By the end of 2005, EiC encompassed 1000 secondary schools and over 1000 primary schools in which the DfES claimed a progressive rise in standards (Kendall and Schagen, 2004). However, an NFER study of results at Key Stages 3 and 4 showed a more equivocal pattern of results. While the policy was generally welcomed and believed to be making a difference, the evidence, in terms of improvements in attainment that could be definitely attributed to EiCs was less clear cut (Kendall, et al., 2005: 50).

Policy, provision and performance at local authority level are determined to a large extent by the population they serve and by the human, social and economic capital available to them. During the Thatcher administration the government began to take an interest in the disparities among local authorities and to question their role in quality assurance and the management of schools in their care. In succeeding years a gradual attrition of local authorities' role took place, but it was down to New Labour to radically recast local authorities as servants of government policy. Whatever their political colour their primary duty would from now on be to promote choice and diversity.

> *Local authorities have longstanding duties to ensure that there are enough school places in their area, and must carry out all their duties to promote high standards. But they have never been charged specifically with promoting choice and diversity in school places, nor ensuring that places are accessible for all. To underpin their role as commissioner of places and champion of pupils and parents, we will place local authorities under a new duty to promote choice, diversity and fair access.*
> (White Paper, DfES, 2005, p. 105)

Local authorities are also enjoined to hold competitions whenever a new school is required; to work actively with promoters who may be parents' groups, education charities backed by business or community or voluntary sector bodies; to develop proposals for Trust or voluntary aided schools; to make their own proposals for self-governing (Foundation) schools, if they cannot find a suitable promoter; to make proposals for the expansion of existing schools, or the addition of specialist SEN facilities; and to encourage and support collaborative working among schools, including independent schools, 'to ensure a seamless pattern of extended services' (DfES, 2005: 96). In some local authorities this takes the form of School Improvement Partnership Boards to oversee school improvement in one or more schools and in cases of failing schools to replace them with an Academy.

What remains at issue is whether the capacity of local authorities, adhering to the canons of choice and diversity, will move towards, or further away from, greater equity. Beneath the rhetoric of schools meeting the 'needs' of pupils, the reality is one in which schools will continue to compete for pupils in order to gain advantage in league table positioning. And there are likely to be penalties for local authorities who do not adhere to the new orthodoxy.

New diversities in forms of schooling

Diversity among forms of schooling has always been a feature of provision in England, whether in the form of a tripartite system, a dual system, or in terms of faith schools, single-sex schools, residential schools, maintained and grant-maintained schools. Moves towards further differentiation were encouraged by the Conservative government in the 1980s who, distrustful of local authorities, encouraged 'opting out'. Among the new variants introduced by the government were City Technology Colleges, invented in 1987 with the chairman of the newly developed CTC Trust, appointed as Adviser to the Secretary of State. A year later the first City Technology College opened, followed in succeeding years by a trickle which by 1994 had become a substantial pool and by the time of the incoming Labour government had become a flood of specialist schools (numbering 245 by the end of 2005). This was much to the dismay of traditional Labour party members who looked for a reversal of Tory polices and witnessed an incoming Labour government not only supporting the specialist school initiative but pledging its expansion.

In 2003 the Trust changed its name to the Specialist Schools Trust to better reflect its work across the specialisms embracing sports, arts and languages colleges. As of September 2005, the Specialist Schools Trust (SST) became the Specialist Schools and Academies Trust (SSAT) in order to signal the Trust's new support role for the Academies programme.

These were to be followed in 2006 by the first cohort of 'trail-blazing' vocational specialist schools with a target of 200 schools becoming vocational specialist schools by 2008. They would play a key role in driving up the numbers of young people achieving level 2 qualifications, with the introduction of the new specialised diplomas and increased post-16 participation rates. Collaboration with partner organisations would offer every young person a rich vocational curriculum and make redundant the 'bog standard' comprehensive school. The concern expressed by professional associations, however, is that for the foreseeable future there will be schools left behind, still on the edge of a brave new world.

Study support

Complementing new forms of provision will be a continuation and expansion of out-of-school hours learning (OSHL). 'Study support' is the generic name given to learning initiatives that take place out of school hours. The DfES document *Extending Opportunity* (first published in 1999 and revised in 2006), describes study support and learning activities outside normal lessons whether they take place on school premises or elsewhere. The visual images and case studies in the DfES document illustrate the whole gamut of outdoor and leisure activities, music, sport, cooking, science and technology, individual work and teamwork, as well as conventional paper and pencil study.

The origins of study support were in local initiatives by schools to provide congenial places for learning, support and mentoring for children and young people from homes in which there was little support or physical space for homework or study. A three year research programme commissioned by the Prince's Trust found that study support could contribute significantly to the three 'A's of attendance, attitude and achievement (MacBeath et al., 2001).

An imaginative offshoot of study support was the Playing for Success initiative, (Sharp et al., 2002) taking study support into football clubs where young people could pursue their learning in surroundings glamorous enough to entice fathers who might never previously have darkened the door of the school. The provision of study support in more relaxed and congenial surroundings, whether in Manchester United's Old Trafford stadium, the community centre or school premises, proved to be a vital complement for schools in areas of disadvantage.

There was a policy logic, therefore, that out of hours learning would become incorporated into the concept of the 'extended school'. While seen by some as simply offering yet more of the same, the 'extended' notion was intended to be an outreach to the other agencies, encapsulating learning as a process of border crossings between school and community.

In 2004, with funds from the National Lottery, £14 million was allocated through the Young People's Fund to the Extended Schools programme in England, focused on schools that served the most disadvantaged areas of the community, including rural disadvantage, addressing the five outcomes of Every Child Matters and involving young people in designing and delivering programme activities.

Extended schools

The government's promise is that by 2010 all secondary schools in England will be open daily from 8 until 6 year round and that by that date all three and four year olds will be entitled to receive 15 hours of free integrated early learning and care for 38 weeks of the year (increasing from the current 12.5 hours) (DfES, 2005b). Parents will have flexibility to use the free entitlement and to purchase additional hours. Extended schools will offer a varied menu of activities including study support, sport (at least two hours a week beyond the school day), music tuition, dance and drama, arts and crafts, special interest clubs such as chess and first aid courses, language, volunteering, business and enterprise activities and visits to places of interest.

Provision for parents and families is integral to the concept of 'extension', including 'swift and easy referral' to specialist support services such as speech therapy, child and adolescent mental health services, family support services, intensive behaviour support, and (for young people) sexual health services. Family learning sessions, would, it was suggested, allow children to learn together with their parents and, in observance of inclusion policies, all children with special educational needs should by right have access to all these services (DfES, 2005).

How far extended schools can be instrumental in raising attainment standards or developing a wider, more liberal and life enhancing agenda remains contested. Given the massive inertia of the 'A to C economy' the counter pressures may be too great (Gillborn and Youdell, 2000). The reference in the 2005 White Paper to 'catch up' and 'stretch' opportunities is perhaps a telling indicator as to their likely fate.

School plus: networking, partnership and collaboration

While holding to the seminal principle of the autonomous school as the unit of comparison, most policy development is now premised on some form of collaboration, networking or partnership – all key words in the new policy lexicon. Excellence in Cities for example, 'is based firmly on the belief that schools working together, collaboratively can achieve more for pupils, parents and communities than schools working in isolation' (Excellence in Cities, p. 30: www. standards. dfes.gov.UK/local/excellence). Collaborative work of this kind is described as 'enhancing performance across an area', offering specialist opportunities within the cluster of schools, 'recognising excellence', 'disseminating good practice'. Similar expansion beyond the autonomous self-improving school is exemplified in *Extended schools* (DfES, 2005c), *Network Learning Communities, Every Child Matters* (DfES, 2004a) and *Youth Matters*, the 14–19 implementation plan and inclusion policies which advocate a more flexible shared form of provision than can be provided by any single school. All of these initiatives assume work beyond school and classroom.

Every Child Matters sets out a national framework for 150 local programmes of change to be led by local authorities and their partners along with a more detailed Outcomes Framework for Inspectorates and other partners 'to inform local needs analysis and the monitoring of progress towards priority targets and indicators' (DfES, 2004a: 1). The mechanism for judging the effectiveness of services (including schools) in meeting children's needs will be through Joint Area Reviews (JARs) covering the range of services provided in the local area. The focus of JARs will be on how those services, both singly and in concert, are working locally to 'improve outcomes' through 'targeted inspection activity explicitly around clear outcomes for children, and focussed on the user, unconstrained by service boundaries' (DfES, 2004a: 1).

Whatever the good intentions of these developments, half a century of initiatives provide evidence of inter-agency work beset with problems. Teachers live in different disciplinary worlds from social workers, community, health and welfare workers whose interventions with young people and families not only take place in very different contexts from institutionalised schooling but are premised on quite different assumptions as to priorities for children and young people. Schools have, historically, been poor at accommodating different frameworks from their own, argues Smith (2005), citing evidence from informal educators experiencing problems when working in schools around issues of confidentiality, discipline, sensitive learning issues and curricular targets. He further argues that informal workers are at a disadvantage in their relationships with school staff because of the authority structures of schools and the prior claims that schools make on young people's goals and priorities.

While the intention of *Every Child Matters* is both ambitious and forward looking, the implications are far reaching and will not be solved simply by admonition or rhetorical gloss.

Diversity at classroom level

The promise of greater diversity in learning and teaching is embodied in 'personalised learning', a big idea which when reduced to its component parts becomes a much more modest concept. The idea was first aired publicly by David Miliband, then Minister for School Standards, in his speech to the North of England Education Conference in January 2005. He defined personalised learning as:

> *High expectations of every child, given practical form by high-quality teaching based on a sound knowledge and understanding of each child's needs. It is not individualised learning where pupils sit alone at a computer. Nor is it pupils left to their own devices, which too often reinforces low aspirations. It can only be developed school by school. It cannot be imposed from above.*

Behind the rhetoric lies something considerably more conservative, leaving most of the conventions of schooling, curriculum and testing untouched. Commissioned by the Specialist Schools Trust to lend weight and substance to this grand idea and turn it into something plausible and practical, David Hargreaves (2004) proposed nine 'gateways':

- student voice;
- curriculum;
- workforce reform;

- mentoring and coaching;
- advice and guidance;
- organisation and design;
- learning to learn;
- assessment for learning;
- new technologies.

It is a list which at face value lacks immediate coherence but sets out to capitalise on strands of promising developments in school practice. At the same time Hargreaves proposed a reframing of the language – personalising', rather than 'personalised' learning, to convey the idea that this was not an end product but a process, 'a learning journey' for both teachers and students.

The Education White Paper, *Higher Standards, Better Schools For All,* offered its own version of a system structured around 'needs'. The word 'tailor' or 'tailored', mentioned 36 times in the document, is used to refer to both customised learning and 'tailored teaching'. It describes personalising as a 'tailored education for every child and young person, that gives them strength in the basics, stretches their aspirations, and builds their life chances' (DfES, 2005b: 50 para 4.1). The promise to parents of 'a tailor-made education for your child' is, apparently, not seen as incompatible with whole-class teaching, a notion which sits oddly with the Hargreaves notion of 'anytime anywhere learning'.

> There is no substitute for high quality whole-class teaching but it needs to be allied with small group or where necessary one-to-one tuition to provide effective support for catch-up. (p. 52)

'Exciting whole-class teaching which gets the best from every child' (p. 45), setting or grouping children of similar ability and attainment, and catch-up for those who fall behind, all signal a system more standardised than personalised, more retrospective than forward looking with 'need', 'interest' and 'choice' ephemeral rather than substantive.

A more genuinely radical version of personalising is outlined in the 2005 Green Paper *Youth Matters*, (DfES, 2005) which argues that not enough is being done to prevent young people from drifting into a life of crime. Young people and their parents, its is proposed, should have a say in what is provided, putting 'spending power' in the hands of young people at risk and disadvantage through a youth opportunity card, giving them discounts for engaging in 'positive activities'. Use of the activity account would link into local databases so as to monitor young people's activities and withhold subsidies when behaviour was unacceptable. The Children's Commissioner, however, has expressed concerns about this aspect of the scheme.

> The small minority who do engage in anti-social behaviour are frequently those who are troubled and come from the most disadvantaged backgrounds. Taking a

punitive approach and withdrawing benefits and incentives would be the very last resort. (Aynsley–Green, 2005: 2)

Schools, for their part, are expected to play a key role in the provision of 'purposeful' opportunities including substantial resourcing for careers guidance and advice, encouraging more peer mentoring, more volunteering and active citizenship in public service, with local youth support teams focusing on preventative work and early intervention with targeted individuals. Responsibility will lie with Children's Trusts and schools for developing services and achieving public service achievement targets around those deemed NEET – not in employment, education or training.

Critics (Delgado, 2002; Davies, 2005; Smith, 2005) counsel caution in too easy an embrace of these proposals, seeing in them a 'big brother' co-option of spontaneity and informal association. They argue that there is an inherent weakness in formalising and institutionalising activity, especially where these seem bent to the service of a curricular agenda or adult inspired outcomes. The focus 'almost exclusively on the individual' (Delgado, 2002: 48) casts young people as individualistic consumers, not citizens.

It is a particularly important challenge for policy in this area to recognise that although the effects of relatively unstructured environments for young people may not be as positive as policy may wish, these may be precisely the contexts in which the most challenging and at-risk young people are choosing to engage. It may be the lack of imposed adult structure and curricula that makes these contexts attractive. Therefore imposing structured activities risks excluding from these programmes precisely the groups targeted. (Feinstein et al., 2005: 18)

The OECD (2004) is also sceptical about expecting to use schools and colleges as policy levers to provide services in social engineering, especially as services tend to be patchy in coverage, accessibility and quality. Their conclusion is echoed by the Select Committee on Education and Skills 2005 (paragraph 99).

Critics of policy making in this area see the long arm of government holding every aspect of personal, social and community life in its powerful embrace. As the tragic case of Victoria Climbié, described in Chapter 1, powerfully illustrates, 'joined-up services' are critical, but many commentators also worry about the erosion of civil liberties, the curtailing of dissent, and the end of spontaneity. One of the key features of good youth work, writes Smith (2005), is that it provides young people with space away from the constant surveillance of families, schools and the state; space to find and be themselves. It might be added that good schools also provide the space for young people to grow in confidence, to challenge orthodoxy and to escape the pervasive imperative of objectives, targets and outcomes.

The limits of policy

In sum, the thrust of much recent policy development has been to expand the range of expectations placed on schools and, in the process, to make the challenge of reforming them still more complex. The fact remains that whilst overall standards may have been slowly rising, no government of whatever political persuasion has yet succeeded in making substantial inroads into levels of inequality between social groups or between the highest- and lowest-performing schools. When they have made progress, it has not usually lasted.

Ball has argued convincingly that change on any scale is unlikely to occur as long as some of the building blocks of educational policy remain unmoved. He identifies three key aspects of policy which frustrate the closing of the achievement gap (2001: 46): 'choice and competition' involving the commodification and consumerisation of education; 'autonomy and performativity' with the managerialisation and commercialisation of education dominating; and 'centralisation and prescription' involving the imposition of centrally determined assessments, schemes of work and classroom methods.

Other commentators (notably Thrupp, 1999) have drawn attention to the limited nature of the assumptions underpinning research on school effectiveness and school improvement. What can be achieved, they have argued, depends entirely on what governments are not merely willing to change but able to bring about. Schools, they suggest, are not entirely powerless but their scope and influence rarely extend beyond the school gates. Furthermore, the willingness to experiment has been dramatically constrained. Even if policy-makers wanted to pursue bold initiatives the menu from which they could choose would, in practice, be rather limited.

Starting points?

Where might policy-makers look for ideas about how to turn round schools in disadvantaged areas? At the turn of the millennium three prominent strands could be identified. The most obvious starting place, perhaps, was the programme already in place for the better part of a decade (and still in place at the time of writing) for schools needing so-called 'Special Measures'. Schools are deemed to require Special Measures if they 'fail' their Ofsted inspections (Ofsted, 1997). They are then required to draw up an action plan and put change strategies in place with a view to being removed from Special Measures within a year.

The Special Measures programme (now renamed 'improvement notice') is not specifically designed, or intended, for schools serving disadvantaged communities although it tends *de facto* to be just this. Schools with high proportions of pupils in receipt of free school meals make up the greater majority of schools in

Special Measures at any one time (Gray, 2000). The driving characteristic behind the approach is that the programme is externally-driven. Inspectors set the agenda and expect those within the school and its community to address a set of common issues: pupil behaviour and expectations, attendance and exclusion, curriculum relevance and 'poor' teaching.

A second prominent strand has involved the development of school improvement from within. Some local authorities have fostered their own approaches whilst others have relied on bringing in help and inspiration from outside. Amongst the latter, one of the most prominent has been the 'Improving the Quality of Education for All' (IQEA) project which aims to enhance student outcomes by focusing on the processes of teaching and learning and by increasing the school's internal capacity for change (Hopkins et al., 1996). In contrast to the Special Measures approach, IQEA places emphasis on conditions for school improvement being in place before the initiative begins, or at least, soon after. There is an expectation that all staff will be consulted, that school co-ordinators will be appointed and that a 'critical mass' of teachers will become actively involved in the work. Crucially, there is an insistence that participating schools make time available for development activities (Hopkins, 2001: 66). At its centre is the assumption that a group of 'school leaders' (drawn from across the school and including some with management responsibilities as well as others in more junior positions) will create the agenda for improvement, the initial impetus and the subsequent drive to keep the school moving forward.

Both the Special Measures and IQEA programmes incorporate the idea that concentrating on a limited number of objectives for concerted action is crucial. This is also a key principle of a third initiative: the High Reliability School (HRS) programme. This developed from knowledge of how 'highly reliable' organisations in other sectors of the economy operate, and aims to impart knowledge about 'what works', engaging staff in extensive training (Reynolds et al., 2001a: Appendix 1). Through close analysis of performance data, identification of 'flaws' in design and 'taking a stand on detail', schools are encouraged to introduce improved practices, set ambitious targets and develop knowledge about 'good practice'.

Notwithstanding their very different starting points, each of these three approaches to school improvement could, by the end of the 1990s, offer evidence of 'success'. Indeed, some of the schools which had either been forcibly enrolled (in the case of Special Measures) or signed up (in the case of IQEA and HRS) could point to substantial progress. Getting an overall picture, however, is more difficult. Not surprisingly, there is an entirely explicable 'bias' in the evidence base towards schools that 'succeeded'. Furthermore, definitions of 'success' vary across the projects. Both considerations can get lost or glossed over in policy discussions. Crucially, none of the programmes ever claimed to have developed strategies

which would work in *almost all* settings. Schools which don't make it to the starting gate for Special Measures, for example, are usually closed down – Special Measures 'works', sooner or later, for schools which stay the course.

There is a related problem in building policy too directly on schools that have become involved with IQEA and HRS. In the former case, where (for whatever reason) the head and teaching staff won't commit themselves wholeheartedly to IQEA's core principles, they tend not to get signed up. Nonetheless, considerable numbers of schools have launched the programme. In the case of HRS a different kind of commitment is needed as it is premised on the 'high reliability organisation', captured in the powerful image of the aircraft control tower for whom a success criterion of 99.9% safe landings would be disastrous. The metaphor is one that does not translate easily into a school setting and any realistic applications to a school context are unlikely to be embraced if school leaders do not make the necessary translation to their own practice.

What are the implications for policy development? Faced with a choice, IQEA is likely to prove more palatable in many schools than either the Special Measures approach, with its heavy emphasis on meeting external demands, or the High Reliability School approach with its distinctive frame of reference. But unfortunately there is another trap that programme designers cannot easily escape: school improvement programmes, of whatever persuasion, have tended to 'work' for those who wanted to make them work. Finally, there was one further stumbling block for policy-makers wanting to launch change on any scale. By the end of the 1990s, none of the UK's apparently more promising school improvement programmes had engaged, systematically and in any depth, with more than a handful of the nation's 'toughest' schools.

Schools in challenging circumstances

These issues also play out in the government programme for schools described as 'facing challenging circumstances'. These were schools conspicuously adrift of the average school performance and showing a growing gulf between them and the highest performing schools. These schools were identified in terms of students' exam performance, 25 per cent or fewer achieving a minimum of five grades A*–C at GCSE, together with 35 per cent or more students entitled to free school meals. Programme criteria summarised on www.standards.dfes.gov.uk/sie/si/SfCC.

In 2005 David Bell, then Chief Inspector of Schools, estimated that the overall number of Schools Facing Challenging Cricumstances (SFCC) had fallen from around 1600 to around 700–800 in 2004 (Office for Standards in Education, 2005). By some sleight of hand the raising of the performance bar above the magic 25% implied that the circumstances surrounding these schools had somehow changed for the better, whereas in truth they may have in many cases got a lot worse. What it does mean is that by targeting, intervention, support and a range of strategic measures these schools had successfully bought into the A–C economy, however temporarily.

Having made some inroads with the SFCCs, the next step for the Government was to set itself an even more ambitious goal: turning the spotlight on schools with an extra 'e' – those schools facing *exceptionally* challenging circumstances (SFECC).

QUESTIONS FOR REFLECTION AND DISCUSSION

1. How would you account for the continuing gap between high and low achievers? And what do you see as the 'levers' most likely to reduce that gap?
2. Are there convincing arguments for developing alternatives to the one-size-fits-all comprehensive school?
3. What can extended schooling do for young people? For their parents?
4. What do you understand by 'personalised learning' and what does it mean for schools on the edge?
5. Can inspection improve schools on the edge?

Note

1   The term, used by Alistair Campbell, was to create much controversy and lead to a Ministerial climb down.

Exceptional Challenges: Schools and Communities on the Edge

The issues raised in the first two chapters are revisited here through the lens of communities and the exceptional challenges which they present to schools on the edge. This chapter examines:

- the new vocabulary of disadvantage;
- how disadvantage translates into quality of life for communities on the edge;
- the contribution of social capital theory to understanding how social exclusion works;
- how staff in schools on the edge have to understand and negotiate two worlds – the intransigent world of educational policy and the turbulent unpredictable world of their local communities.

The discourse of disadvantage

The language used to describe disadvantage has, with each passing decade, been revisited and re-formed, both to provide a more accurate conceptual rendering and also to soften the more abrasive political edge which locates schools as victims of systemic discrimination. In an era when headteachers' bookshelves contain titles such as *Strategic Marketing for Schools* (Davies and Ellison, 1996) and the DfES website offers advice on how to market your school (DfES, 2006), the label a school carries can make all the difference to its chances for survival. The application of terms such as 'Academy' to describe schools serving peculiarly disadvantaged communities appears as a political sleight of hand in what Alterman (2005) characterises as the 'post-truth political environment', a media saturated society in which the margin between 'truth' and 'untruth' is harder to discern beneath artful spin and judicious presentation.

The terminology of schools 'in challenging circumstances', applied by government to schools with attainment below what is deemed to be the acceptable threshold, may be read as one such euphemism designed to obscure the reality of schools serving poor neighbourhoods. In 2000, secondary schools were set a series of stepped targets for minimum performance at GCSE. The minimum targets were 20% for 2004 and 25% for 2006. Any schools in 2000 with 25% 5 A*–C at GCSE or less, along with some schools with 35% or more eligibility for free school meals, were described as 'facing challenging circumstances', provided with extra funding, resources and support and monitored by Her Majesty's Inspectors (HMI). In 2000, 480 mainstream secondary schools were judged to fall into this category (DfES, 2001b).

An even newer intensification of the terminology has been developed for schools in which performance levels are judged at first glance to be in a virtually terminal condition. These are 'schools in *exceptionally* challenging circumstances'. This term came into usage with the launch by the DfES of the SFECC Project in 2001, a shorthand for what were originally designated as Schools Facing Extremely Challenging Circumstances. Later on the word 'extremely' was replaced with 'exceptionally', a descriptor perhaps seen as less contentious. These eight schools, chosen for concentrated intervention over a three year period, fell so far outside the normal parameters of achievement that they were therefore seen as 'exceptions' to the rule. The Project was predicated on the notion that one could distinguish between an unsuccessful school and a school for the unsuccessful. The latter, it was assumed could be turned round with good leadership and appropriate forms of external support, encouragement and resourcing. It was an idea put sternly to the test, as what little we know about schools on the edge is that they are defined to a large extent by the communities they serve.

Communities on the edge

What are the challenges facing communities on the edge? As we have argued in the preceding chapters, what happens outside schools is more telling for achievement than what happens within them, a recurring finding of many of the school effectiveness studies outlined in Chapter 1. The evidence has been remarkably consistent over the four decades since Coleman et al. (1966) and Jencks et al. (1972) reported on inequality as rooted in systemic factors which divide families and communities. In England the significance of social background has most recently been demonstrated in data on the attainment gap at GCSE between children with parents in managerial or professional occupations and those with parents in unskilled manual occupations. The differential has, for a decade, remained stubbornly at a level of around 44 to 45% (National Statistics, 2005).

While child poverty has fallen as a result of the increase in employment since 1997 (Palmer et al., 2005), income in the UK has gone down and is concentrated in communities which are pushed to the outer edge of the economic mainstream. 50% of those on low incomes live in 20% of small local areas and 50% of primary school children who qualify for free school meals are concentrated in 20% of schools. In ex-manufacturing areas, the decrease in the demand for low skilled workers has compounded disadvantages for people, particularly men, with no qualifications. Disadvantaged groups are more likely to be economically inactive than the population as a whole, a situation which then impacts in a cumulative way on every other index of disadvantage. As Brighouse has pointed out, in urban areas 'there is a chronic and acute shortage of permanent jobs for the unskilled and the semi-skilled, especially for those for whom strength and motor skills are important' (1996: 120). Webster et al., in their study of the transitions in life of the poor, similarly comment on the lack of appropriate employment in poor neighbourhoods.

> *Current policy emphasises supposed deficits in employability and skills among marginalised adults. This is to be rectified by training, advice, incentives and child-care support. However, this marginal redistribution of income and opportunity will not lift people out of poverty, unless they have access to good quality training and rewarding and secure employment. Poor training and poor employment opportunities tend to be synonymous. Income from decent rather than poor work, for those able to work, is the best way of lifting people out of poverty.* (2004: 43)

Households in disadvantaged areas have fewer amenities, such as central heating or washing machines, and are less likely to have access to their own form of transport. In 2001–02, 86% of households in Great Britain in the highest income group had access to a home computer, almost six times as many as for households in the lowest income group. The gap was even wider for Internet connections which give access not only to information but to social contacts beyond the immediate neighbourhood (National Statistics, 2005).

Challenges such as these impact on a day-to-day basis on individuals and families in communities on the edge. It is in the interplay of these facets of disadvantage that we see the erosion of people's sense of self worth and self-efficacy and we get some insight into how those perceptions transfer themselves intergenerationally. Physical and mental health on the one hand, and intellectual and emotional disposition on the other, are not simply correlated but causally linked. Health, in turn, is related causally to the quality of housing (space, dampness, sanitation, safety), to the availability of transport and car ownership in emergencies, to information and people's confidence to deal with bureaucracies and professionals. Kearns and Parke (2003) point out that in relation to amenities and quality of life, the expectations of residents in poor areas are the same as those in more affluent ones. They are equally concerned with poor housing, street noise, crime, vandalism – 'they just experience those conditions more often than others' (2003: 23).

> Indeed, poor area is a significant predictor of unhappiness with both disorder in the surroundings and with the surrounding environment, which is not surprising given that certain problems such as a poor general appearance and higher levels of vandalism are more prevalent in poor areas. (837)

The influence of social capital

The complex interweave of circumstance is encapsulated in social capital theory which examines the pattern and intensity of networks among people, the support they receive from those networks and the sense of well-being and empowerment that they derive from shared values and the trust they have in their environment. The OECD definition of social capital is 'networks together with shared norms, values and understandings that facilitate co-operation within or among groups' (Cote and Healy, 2001: 41). The concept is operationalised in three key measures – trust, social membership and access to networks.

Levels of trust are measured by whether individuals trust their neighbours, whether they consider their neighbourhood a place where people help each other or the degree of apprehension about local people who are seen to pose a threat.

Social membership is measured by the number of organisations, clubs, societies or social groups to which an individual belongs.

Access to networks is measured in terms of people's ability to make and maintain links in informal situations which offer friendship and support outside of formal organisations. These may be casual or short term ('weak links') or close personal relationships ('strong links') which develop through extended families, neighbourhoods, local associations and in a range of informal and formal meeting places.

National data (National Statistics, 2005) reveal significant differences in membership of organisations, in face-to-face and virtual networks between the most and least privileged. Union affiliation, the most likely organisation for membership among lower income groups has seen a continuous decline in membership over the last decade. Social trust, as measured by perceptions of neighbourhood, violence, crime and casual contacts is also markedly lower in disadvantaged communities. A key discriminator is whether there are people one can turn to in a crisis. While the more privileged frequently enjoy wide networks of support, both emotionally and economically, many people in disadvantaged neighbourhoods report having few people, and in some cases no one, to turn to who can be of material help. Webster et al. (2004: 30) report the extent to which strong bonds, particularly amongst family members, are critical for coping with life in poor communities but that these strong networks, if they exclude outsiders and the unknown, can severely constrain freedoms and opportunities. Strong social networks can also draw individuals into crime and drug use.

Research has shown that higher levels of social capital are associated with better health, better employment outcomes, lower crime rates and higher educational achievement (see for example Putnam, 2000). Those with extensive networks are more likely not only to be housed, healthy, hired and happier but also more willing and able to access and find success within the educational system.

The frequency and quality of contact, and the strength of bonding between people, is an important discriminator. Social capital theory uses three explanatory concepts which help to deepen insights into the importance of formal and informal networks.

Bonding social capital is characterised by strong bonds, for example among family members or among members of the same ethnic group which help in 'getting by' in life. For many disadvantaged individuals or groups the security of having family to call on is an invaluable social and educational resource. Strong social bonding, whether within the family or in friendship groups, religious sects, clubs or gangs can, however, be an inhibiting factor, cutting people off from wider social contacts which may offer alternative perspectives.

Bridging social capital is the avenue of escape from insular and inward-looking association. Social bridging is seen in the connections made with other people who stand outside the immediate reference group and its value orientations. These are often 'weak links', casual and informal but cutting across social and ethnic affiliations, exposing one to differing lifestyles, value systems and occupational groups. Bridging may also be virtual in nature, in which people establish links with others on a national and international basis via the Internet. These forms of linkage open up new worlds, new ways of seeing, and new ways of relating and learning. While relatively inexpensive they are beyond the budget of the most disenfranchised groups and rely not only on access to relevant technologies but the ability and confidence to use them to advantage.

Linking social capital is a form of bridging that describes a different kind of social network. While social bridging is collegial and 'horizontal' in nature, linking social capital works on the vertical plane, that is, within hierarchies of power and influence. Being able to make, and use, connections with people in positions of power and authority can prove to be the key to accessing vital resources – financial, social, and educational. How these theoretical constructs play out in practice is illustrated in the following critical incident affecting an inner-city

London family. At each point in the story we may stop and ask: what could have been different had there been a stronger legacy of linking and bridging social capital?

CASE STUDY

Anouka

Playing too close and too inquisitively with D-I-Y electrical wiring, Anouka was subject to an intense electric shock and severe burns to her right arm. Her mother, in panic, knocked on a neighbour's door and then on another to see if she could borrow some cream or bandages to put on the child's burn, or perhaps an aspirin to stop the pain. Neither neighbour was willing to open a front door at that time of night. As Mrs Okede's phone had been cut off she was unable to call her estranged husband, now living at the other end of the city. She decided she would take Anouka to the casualty department of the nearest hospital. With Anouka in her arms she walked the quarter mile to the bus stop where she knew there would be late running buses. She was lucky as one came within fifteen minutes and took her quite close to the hospital. The receptionist there was sympathetic to the child's clear distress but advised Mrs Okede that this was the wrong hospital and gave her directions to another hospital two miles away. Two bus rides and an hour later mother and child arrived at the casualty department of the second hospital where they waited patiently in an overcrowded room for Anouka to be seen.

There are many points at which, with knowledge, self confidence, social networks, and taken-for-granted infrastructures a much simpler story could have been told and one that could have been quite easily resolved. Such incidents, all too familiar in life on the edge, may, however, have little connection with schooling, wrapped up in its own concerns. From a community perspective those priorities may be seen as trivial in the wider scheme of things.

Social capital and schooling

The same concepts of bonding, bridging and vertical linking apply powerfully within a school context. School education requires each of these in some balanced measure, and in successful schools young people are helped to achieve a balance among them. School is a place in which social bonding begins to take shape from virtually day one and may grow stronger all the way through primary and secondary school and into adulthood, and even into lifelong partnership. But this can work either to the school's advantage or to its detriment. The bonding of pro-school groups and anti-school groups has long been the subject of illuminating research (see for example Hargreaves, 1967; Willis, 1977), illustrating how strong in-group affiliations can often work at cross purposes to the norms and values that schools attempt to instil. Since it was first identified by Coleman and his team in 1966, school effectiveness research over the following four decades has continued to document the impact of 'the compositional effect' (or peer group effect) as a key variable in distinguishing more effective from less effective schools (MacBeath and Mortimore, 2001). As teachers know without needing recourse to research, when there is strong bonding within groups, particularly gangs with their own sworn allegiances, they may prove highly resistant to the best intentions of teachers to engage their interest or change their belief systems.

Grammar and secondary modern schools encouraged their own forms of bonding, reinforcing a social and academic divide. The creation of comprehensive schools may be seen as an attempt to effect social bridging, in the belief that young people would achieve better in a 'mixed ability' environment and that benefits would be seen in personal and social education, citizenship and career opportunities. Some hoped that if there were a social, ethnic and gender mix it would broaden horizons and allow young people to become familiar with different lifestyles and cultures. These seminal principles have been seriously undermined, however, by market-driven policies and back door selection which allow 'bridging social capital' to be drained off from schools, affecting not only the student 'balance' within the school but depriving it of the parents most able to give indirect and direct support.

'Linking social capital' is reduced where there is an imbalance in the educational background of parents, their knowledge and confidence in supporting their children and their willingness to visit and participate in school affairs. 'Doing school' successfully requires both young people and their parents to be able to engage successfully with hierarchies and authorities and to negotiate their paths through school conventions. As has been demonstrated by work within the National Youth Agency (Wylie, 2004), young people from more privileged backgrounds owe much of their success to their ability to navigate within the system with an understanding of the rules and the safety blanket of home support. Reduced ability and confidence of parents to deal with hospital receptionists, welfare agencies, or police result in frustrations and alienation which may be passed on consciously, or insidiously, to their children.

Social capital theory helps us to gain a better understanding of attitudes to school learning when we extend our line of sight from school to community, to the local living environment, to housing and social services, employment opportunities, health and crime levels. Extending sight lines brings into view the texture of life as it is lived out of school, the belated recognition that for 'those in deprived areas […] there is a real lack of interesting, accessible and affordable things to do.' (DfES 2004a: 61). The link between leisure activities available to young people and adult outcomes is of growing significance for researchers (for example Feinstein et al., 2005). The OECD's PISA Report (2004: 208) concludes that many aspects of educational disadvantage are not amenable to education policy and that it is only in the longer term, with a rise in the educational achievement of parents and wider economic development, that the attainment gap will be reduced. This is not, however, simply a counsel of despair, as one of the main messages from that same report is that the closer policy and practice are to the learner, the greater the likelihood of impact. The more classroom-bound the focus, the less the potential for nurturing deep learning. The more insulated the experience from 'real life', the less likelihood there is of penetrating the inner world of disenfranchised young people.

These issues about family and peer groups and their inter-relationship with schools are of great significance because peer group norms and mores are not always kept outside the school gates. They impinge, sometimes in dramatic fashion, on the lives of classrooms. The answers are not likely to lie in more structured class teaching, in tighter objectives, or even in a more radical restructuring of the curriculum, but in imaginative approaches to informal learning, more informed and creative inter-agency work, alertness to local social issues and greater proactivity in addressing them.

What we know about schools on the edge

As we have argued, schools on the edge face distinctive challenges about which we have still much to learn. The rich seam of literature in the United States is not matched in Britain where little empirical data is available on schools at the critical edge of social and economic challenge. By the very fact that these schools are in 'exceptional' circumstances, generalisations do not apply. Improvement strategies such as Improving the Quality of Education for All and High Reliability Schools, described in Chapter 2, rely on internal capacity building but their inherent weakness is a failure to address the dynamic relationships between these schools and their communities. Improvement cannot be fully explored without constant reference to the context in which these schools are situated and their capacity to reach out to, and engage with, their local communities. Educational improvement in its broadest sense means building bridges between school and the world of family, community and external social agencies. For MacGilchrist, 'school improvement is not a linear, continuous, upward trajectory' (2003: 32). It will, she concludes, continue to defy prescription unless new and more sophisticated ways are devised to shift away from the present deficit model.

While there are many worthwhile lessons to be drawn from effectiveness and improvement studies, it cannot be assumed that the defining characteristics of an effective school can be applied to make an ineffective school more effective, especially if that school faces multiple disadvantages (Barber, 1996; Stoll and Myers, 1998). Many of their starting points differ from schools more in the mainstream; differences which are made manifest from the earliest stages. Often by the time children enter Year 7 they have not achieved levels high enough to be able to engage in any meaningful way with the Key Stage 3 curriculum, often because, from a bad start there has been little opportunity to catch up. Learning may be subject to a series of disruptions – temporary residence in different localities, transitions among several previous schools, frequent absenteeism through ill health, and exclusion as a consequence of an inability to cope with the demands of schooling. Many are children of refugees, asylum seekers and migrant workers, their low attainment at Key Stage 2 SATs explained by the fact that they are still learning English.

When the defining characteristic of a school is the volatility and turbulence of its local communities, the impact on the internal culture is evident in every aspect of school and classroom life. Learning is never a simple matter of building on what went before. To learn well and to teach well relies on a minimal level of stability of pupil, parent and teacher population. Teaching has to have some consistency of focus; learning requires coherence and continuity, not only between life in school and out of school but within those precious and fragmented classroom interludes in which teachers try to sustain a relationship of trust, optimism and perseverance. The greater the pressures in young people's lives, the higher the absenteeism and discontinuity in their classroom learning. The greater the stress on teachers, the less their health and consistency of attendance can be assured. The more under-resourced the school as a whole, the greater the demands which stretch the capacity and capability of the teaching force. The higher the demand for teacher in-service professional development, the more likely teachers are to be absent from the classroom, perhaps at critical junctures in the learning/teaching cycle.

A report by the OECD (2003: 21) referred to a 'low sense of belonging' which, they concluded, was experienced by up to a quarter of 15-year-olds in schools, not just in England but in many other countries, due to a general failure to find viable alternatives to the traditional progression route which has proved too insurmountable a hurdle for many young people. In England, as Tomlinson et al. (2004) have argued, GCSEs were originally designed for 40% of the population, not as an accountability lever or as a valid measure of school effectiveness. In England, participation in formal learning post-16 is lower than in comparable countries with only 84% of 16-year-olds in formal education or work based learning (DfES, 2004a) while the DfES and Learning Skills Council are, writes Foster (2005: 48), 'failing to provide an integrated and coherent view' of alternatives for young learners.

In short, for schools on the edge it is impossible to rely on some of the core assumptions as to what constitutes 'good practice' and, as a result, many of the prescriptions for improvement break down. For an improvement culture to take root a number of essential preconditions have to be met.

Edging towards stability

Recruitment

The first and most essential premise is a full staffing complement. The Catch 22 is, of course, that it is in these less attractive schools that the 'crisis' in recruitment and retention of teachers bites hardest. While the issue is a national one it is also highly discriminatory in its impact.

The Select Committee on Education and Employment's Ninth Report to Parliament (House of Commons, 1998) expressed serious concern about the failure to attract people into teaching. A 2002 report by the General Teaching Council in Wales (GTCW) reported a crisis in teacher recruitment with one in ten posts remaining unfilled. Its chief executive claimed that 'clearly heads don't believe they have enough choice of applicants to make the appointments they want ... In some cases, they had no choices at all' (p. 8). Despite various initiatives the problem remains. The House of Commons Select Committee on Education and Skills, reporting in 2004, remarked:

> *High turnover, and the inability of some schools to recruit sufficient high calibre teachers, has a knock on effect on the achievement of pupils in those schools. Turnover within the profession may not be a significant issue for schools in general; but for those schools in the most challenging circumstances it can exacerbate an already difficult situation.* (House of Commons, 2004: 16)

The crisis in attracting headteachers to disadvantaged areas is equally acute. A series of studies using NFER data (Earley et al., 1990; Earley et al., 1995; Earley et al., 2002) reported a generally low response to headship advertisements, varying according to geographical region and school phase. It was shown that applicants for primary headship ranged from 0 to 156 and those for secondary headship from 6 to 200. For special schools the figures were between 1 and 80.

Howson's 2003 study for the National College of School Leadership found that, on average, primary schools in London received only five applications for each headteacher post, and only 5% of London primary schools received more than ten applications; 98% of London primary schools interviewed no candidates at all and 63% of schools surveyed in London had to re-advertise compared to 25% in the Home Counties and 22% elsewhere. Regional variations were little different in the secondary sector. While 62% of secondary schools in the Home Counties and 57% in other regions received 20 or more applications, in London the figure was 29%. The range of applications from school to school throws into sharp relief the differential attractiveness of jobs in different parts of the country and in varying locations.

The recruitment crisis for schools in 'less desirable' circumstances is exacerbated in areas of the country where the cost of living has become particularly high. These factors apply most acutely in London boroughs. Indeed, 'London Issues', the problems faced by schools in attracting enough teachers to London schools, became a focus for the DfES Standards Task Force in 2000. In 2001 the DfES announced the setting up of a Teacher Recruitment and Retention Fund targeted on 'schools in high cost or challenging areas' (DfES, 2001c), with strategies such as bursaries, housing allowances and golden hellos in shortage subjects. In the House of Commons Select Education and Skills Committee, in 2004, the Minister of State acknowledged the depth of the problem:

> *I have to be very careful about saying something is adequate because I think it is very challenging ... We have to accept that we are fighting against some pretty strong market forces in terms of London housing. We are making a fist of it, but it is tough. I certainly would not claim victory in this area.* (House of Commons, 2004: 29)

Teacher and headteacher recruitment are clearly inter-related and the new pressures on headship explain the low rate of teachers willing to apply for posts. The headteacher role has been further diminished by the need to resort to poaching, headhunting, using temporary staff from agencies, filling vacancies with short term contracts for Australian, South African or Canadian teachers, or employing other 'innovative' means to fill vacant posts. This requires a large investment of time and emotional energy and takes heads and other staff out of their schools, distracting them from other priorities. In short, disadvantage has its own unique pressures. As one primary head remarked, people working in such schools need:

> *Super-human strength, a real commitment that is almost a vocation, being stubborn, prepared to fight for what you think is right ... raising expectations of pupils, parents and at times, staff ... humour, ability to cope with angry parents and the tenacity ... the real battle ... to get those people who don't work with children in a community like this to understand what we are doing.* (Headteacher, Octet feeder primary school)

The tragic ending of the life of one headteacher, a middle-aged family man with a mission to help poor young black teenagers through 'tough love', became a story about the failure of education to compensate for challenging circumstances and the heartbreak which can await those who try. What transpired in the last decade of St George's School, Maida Vale is a story which illustrates some of the bleakness of the downward forces affecting schools in poor neighbourhoods.

Exceptional challenge: St George's story

St George's is the Roman Catholic comprehensive school where, in 1995, its headteacher Philip Lawrence was stabbed to death at the school gates, protecting a 13-year-old black pupil from attack by a 15-year-old member of a black gang from a rival school. The school stumbled into decline and in 2000 failed its Ofsted inspection. It was even closed for a period because of violence inside the school gates. Mr Lawrence's replacement took early retirement after a student was injured in a gang fight in which a classroom and a teacher's car were damaged.

Westminster Council then gave the school one year to come off the list of failing schools, and the school was reopened and re-energised under a new headteacher Lady Marie Stubbs who was coaxed out of retirement to turn the school round. This period in the school's history became the stuff of positive media headlines – and a television production in which Marie Stubbs was played by Julie Walters in the ITV drama 'Ahead of the Class'. Stubbs said at the time:

> If we are talking about what is called 'a cycle of deprivation', I think not to believe this can be broken is a counsel of despair and no sensible teacher can subscribe to a belief in the inevitability of a cycle of deprivation … All our professional training and sense of vocation, particularly in the Catholic sector of course but not exclusively, leads us to believe that positive intervention can bring about change, and that's what I want to see happening in St George's. (BBC broadcast 29 July 2006)

Her stay was characterised as a new beginning. Bob Marley music was piped through the school and Lenny Henry and Cherie Blair came to call. Having retired, she never planned to stay long and was succeeded by Philip Jakszta, the former acting head of a Catholic school in Tower Hamlets, after governors overlooked her deputy, Sean Devlin, the man she wanted to replace her. Mr Jakszta won a glowing report for the school from Ofsted, and praise for his leadership. But he in turn has now quit, leaving the school, in the Autumn term 2005, without a full-time head (*Independent* Online November 25, 2005) http://education.independent. co.uk/news/article 329178.ece. There are now plans to turn the school into an Academy.

There are heroic stories of schools which are apparently turned round by visionary heads such as Lady Stubbs, but all too often the story is one without a sequel because sustainability has never been part of the equation and external forces are then allowed to push schools back to the place from where they came. The nature of this process is chronicled by Fink (1999) in his studies of the ways in which a slow process of attrition affects the most bold and radical attempts to change the status quo.

The statistics of disadvantage

The battle against attrition is the natural state of schools on the edge, statistics for which only touch the surface of the issues. These are, however, a useful starting point for probing further and deeper. A recent DfES account lays out six key indicators:

1. Schools serving areas of severe socio-economic disadvantage.
2. Schools with a high proportion of pupils with special educational needs.
3. Schools whose pupils have low prior attainment, poor motivation and low self-esteem.
4. Schools with a high proportion of transient pupils.
5. Schools where many of the pupils speak languages other than English.
6. Schools whose past reputation has made it difficult to maintain pupil numbers and consequently sufficient staff to offer a high quality education (DfES, 2004b: www.standards.dfes.gov.uk).

Eligibility for free school meals (FSM) is a much used but simplistic and inadequate proxy for disadvantage. Nonetheless its inverse relationship with educational attainment at secondary level attests to a deeper malaise. While nearly half of all 16-year-olds fail to gain five or more GCSEs at grade C or above, the figure rises to three quarters of those students who are eligible for free school meals. Furthermore, there is clear evidence of clustering. If you are a secondary school student who qualifies for a free school meal, your school averages 25% FSM eligibility; if you are not, your school averages 12% (Palmer et al., 2005: 42). Poverty and low attainment walk hand in hand: 11-year-old students on free school meals are twice as likely not to have achieved Level 4 at KS2 as other 11-year-old students (p. 35).

There are other ways in which poverty exerts its influence on a school's social mix. Research by the Sutton Trust into the top 200 comprehensive schools in England in terms of 5+ A*–C at GCSE found evidence of an inherent and insidious social divide at work (2006: 2). The study aimed 'to discover the extent to which pupils eligible for FSM do – or do not – attend high performing state schools when academic selection is not a factor' (p. 3) and they found:

> *Social selection is evident in top comprehensive schools: the overall proportion of pupils eligible for free school meals at the 200 highest performing comprehensives is 5.6%, compared to 11.5% of children in the postcode sectors of the schools, and 14.3% in secondary schools nationally.* (p. 2)

These high performing comprehensive schools could not, officially at least, select pupils but, as the Sutton study shows, attainment and affluence are bound together. There is selection by overt or covert means in schools, even in schools in which this runs counter to policy. The postcode data have particular significance because children next door to one another end up in different schools, as it is the more affluent or informed families in that neighbourhood whose children attend the highest performing, ostensibly 'non selective' comprehensive schools.

These insights are of critical importance for the study of schools serving poor neighbourhoods. In all of these schools there is a systemic downward inertia. Without local support and a strong and consistent set of forces working in the opposite direction these schools would simply concede to attrition and entropy. External support is critical to their survival, but it needs to be relevant and powerful enough to vouchsafe longer term sustainability.

Ethnicity and the reality of racism

Data on ethnicity demonstrate further the multi-layered nature of disadvantage but also conceal deeper issues of racism. There is no inherent hierarchy of intelligence and ability among different ethnic groups but in secondary schools in England, all major ethnic groups outperform Black Caribbean students who also, not coincidentally, are the ethnic group most 'on the edge' of the mainstream – socially and economically.

An Ofsted study of all 129 schools in England with more than a 10% Black Caribbean student population found that they were distinguished by the following characteristics:

- the average proportion of Black Caribbean pupils was 17%, compared to 1.4% in secondary schools nationally;
- most of these schools served areas of relatively high socioeconomic deprivation, with almost two thirds of the schools having more than 35% of pupils eligible for free school meals, and only five schools with eligibility below the national average;
- the majority were in inner and outer London LEAs, with the rest in metropolitan and unitary authorities. (Ofsted, 2002: 33)

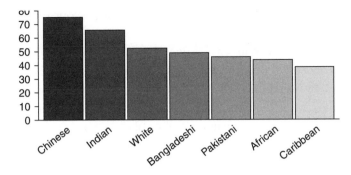
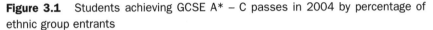

Figure 3.1 Students achieving GCSE A* – C passes in 2004 by percentage of ethnic group entrants

Source: DfES 2005, GCSE results, England 2004, National Statistics, First Release SFR 08/2005 (24 February 2005) www.dfes.gov.uk.rsgateway/DB/SFR

In discussions of race and achievement, often conducted in simplistic terms, the complexities of class, gender and geographical location tend to be ignored (Mirza, 2005). Schools with high proportions of minority ethnic pupils and those with English as an additional language (EAL) tend to be located within areas where there is relative social deprivation and, unsurprisingly, performance levels in these areas are relatively low. There are strong associations between the percentage of pupils with English as an additional language and the proportion of pupils eligible for FSM, with high proportions on one measure corresponding with high proportions on the other.

Getting at the underlying difficulties, however, can be problematic. Owen et al. (2000) point to the fact that at GCSE level, schools with higher proportions of pupils with EAL, appeared to have higher performances overall than other schools with equivalent levels of FSM, and suggest that it is possible that EAL is a shorter-term issue for learning, whereas FSM is a more constant indicator of disadvantage. This is a judgment echoed in part by Lupton (2004a; 2004b) who draws attention to important differences in the attitudes of different ethnicities and cultures to education, suggesting that for white working class disadvantaged communities, education in previous generations was not an important consideration. By contrast other parents, for example from Chinese or Indian backgrounds, while equally disadvantaged economically and socially often value education as a means of making progress in society and have higher expectations of their children. However, Mirza highlights the dangers of this kind of distinction based on ethnic and cultural 'differences'.

In the new cultural construction of 'race', cultural and religious difference is played out when we say '... blacks are good at sport, not so good at school. Chinese are good at maths, and make good food. Asians are good at business and love family life. Muslims cannot be trusted: they are aggressive, sexist and, under all those clothes, usually a bit wild-eyed'. Racism in this cultural and religious guise seems less overt. (2005: 6)

The phrase 'institutionalised racism' has entered the discourse as a result of the inquiry into the death of Stephen Lawrence, a promising young black student who was stabbed to death at a south-east London bus stop in April 1993 by a white gang shouting racist abuse. No one has been convicted of the murder despite the ongoing battle for justice by his parents. The Metropolitan Police were found to have bungled the investigation, and '[t]he conclusion reached by the inquiry chairman Sir William Macpherson [was] that police prejudice against black people was so ingrained that it contributed to allowing racist murderers to get away with their crime' (Dodd, 2000).

What has also become established through the Macpherson report is the definition of racism – that it can be discrimination unwittingly and without intent. A racist incident is defined as 'any incident which is perceived to be racist by the victim or any other person'. An illustration of this comes from Youdell (2003: 16) describing how, during a school assembly in which there was no apparent disruption, black boys were singled out and ejected from the hall. This was not because the head of year was deliberately discriminating against them but because, implicitly, these boys were identified in this community as a group who challenge authority.

CASE STUDY

Black bodies walking, Year 11 Assembly

Source: Youdell, 2003: 16

The majority of the year group (predominantly white), group tutors (all white, predominantly women), and DY are present.

The head of year (man, white) is addressing the year group. The head of year pauses and looks out to the back of the assembled students. A few minutes later, looking in the same part of the audience, he calls out a short string of boys' names and instructs them to pay attention. A minute or so later he stops mid-sentence and calls: 'OK Daniel, outside my office please'. There is a pause. Daniel (boy, black) slowly gets to his feet, shaking his head as he does so. He takes his time as he leaves the hall, there is a sway and spring to his gait. The head of year continues his address. Through the rest of the address the head of year sends a further two black boys from the same group to wait outside his office. Each boy exits in a similar manner to Daniel. As the final boy walks towards the door, the head of year continues to chastise him. The boy makes a short tutting sound, which is audible to those towards the front of the hall, as he walks out of the door.

In 2002, the rate of exclusion of Black Caribbean students was three times higher than that for white students and twenty times the rate for Chinese and Indian students. Whereas 71% of Chinese students achieved 5+ A*–C grades, the figure for Black Caribbean boys was 25% whilst for white students the figure was 46%. But when social class is added to the equation the figures for white students drop significantly. Gillborn and Mizra (2000) give a finer grained picture of attainment within the black ethnic group between pupils from non-manual and manual backgrounds, showing that class differences in patterns of attainment for white pupils are replicated among black young people. This plays out too in the targeting of students who are seen as most likely to improve the school's performance statistics with black students, particularly boys, finding themselves in the 'low ability' sets (Gillborn and Youdell, 2000).

This is not the place to disentangle the interaction between class and race, but there are worrying signs that some ethnic groups have missed out on the overall trends in performance. Though there is some evidence of improvement for example the rate of exclusion among Black Caribbean students has halved (Palmer et al., 2005: 35), in some cases the inequalities have increased in recent years: African-Caribbean and Pakistani pupils, for example, have not shared equally in the rising levels of GCSE attainment (Gillborn and Mirza, 2000: 27).

The inclusion enigma

It is these low performing schools, in the most challenging of circumstances, that are at the sharp end of the inclusion agenda. The policy is for children and young people who would previously have been on the edge of the mainstream, in special schools, to be 'included' in mainstream schools along with their same age peers. This principle is one that teachers have mostly welcomed but in practice it has brought a new raft of problems, particularly for schools 'facing challenging circumstances' in which there are disproportionate percentages of students with special educational needs (SEN). In January 2005 almost 242,600 pupils (nursery, primary, secondary) in England had statements of SEN, and 60% of these students were in mainstream schools, but concentrated in relatively few schools: over 70% of primary schools and 44% of secondary had less than 2% of pupils with statements of SEN. Less than 1% of both primary and secondary schools had over 10% of pupils with statements. The incidence of special educational needs (with or without statements) is much higher for boys than for girls. Statemented SEN students were nine times more likely to be excluded than those with 'no SEN'. There was a strong and consistent link between exclusion, truancy and achievement. SEN (unlike eligibility for FSM) is defined and funded by the local authority. So, besides any pressures to reduce the numbers of SEN students for central political purposes, there are very real funding advantages to an authority for setting the bar high for establishing SEN.

In the battle for ratings schools are reluctant to accept young people who will drag down performance scores and are happy to see them accommodated by a neighbouring school with an already generous complement of SEN pupils. Berliner (2006) describes a process of commodification whereby children and young people come to be seen as 'score enhancers' or 'score detractors'. The impact of policies which treat pupils as unit measures pushes disadvantaged schools closer to the edge, to the edge of special measures or to an 'improvement notice', and possibly ultimate closure. A recent study of inclusion described the double disadvantage for these schools.

> *In disadvantaged areas where a school may have over half its pupils classified as 'special needs' and five or more per cent of children statemented, strategies which may work in more stable situations do not apply. Here the critical 'balance' shifts so as to make effective teaching nigh on impossible. It is only with exceptional dedication and resilience that teachers cope with the turbulence and unpredictability of day-to-day life. It is in these circumstances that lack of resources and insufficient expertise issues hit hardest.* (MacBeath et al., 2006: 34)

This study reported not only the impact on schools, but on teachers and on pupils themselves struggling to make sense of a curriculum that made no sense. These pupils were typically given into the full-time care of teaching assistants who, with goodwill but without expertise, watered down the curriculum so that these young people could grasp something of the importance to their lives of Boudica, the Saxons, geometry and soil erosion. Florian and Rouse (2001) have shown the pernicious effects on attitudes to children with special needs, caught in tensions between the two agendas – standards and needs. Pressures on teachers to meet curriculum targets not only shape staff attitudes to special needs but extend to parents and pupils too, who begin to resent the diversion of teachers' energies and priorities. In the process, two laws – the legal and moral – are undermined. The law which forbids discrimination against children goes hand in hand with 'the law of natural distribution' which expects schools to take an equitable share of children with special needs.

SEN interacts with poverty, albeit in complex ways. Despite government and research suggesting that it is classless, there is a high coincidence of SEN and FSM – about a quarter of those with SEN were eligible for free school meals compared with 12% of those without SEN. Schools concerned with doing well in the examination performance tables have done their best to avoid too many of these students, while others deserted by middle class parents because of their lower league position, have taken additional numbers in order to claim the available resources in an effort to balance the budget and retain viable staffing levels

(Tomlinson, 2004). Schools become well-known locally for being good with SEN students and local authorities can become complicit in directing SEN students to these schools – particularly when they are less popular locally and would otherwise be under-subscribed. The most prevalent type of SEN amongst pupils with statements of SEN in secondary and special schools is Moderate Learning Difficulty, 29% and 30% respectively (MacBeath et al., 2006).

Warnock, who chaired the influential commission in 1978 which gave us the term 'SEN', now accepts that too may different kinds of need and disability are shoehorned into one all-embracing term.

> *The idea of transforming talk of disability into talk of what children need has turned out to be a baneful one. If children's needs are to be assessed by public discussion and met by public expenditure it is absolutely necessary to have ways of identifying not only what is needed but also why (by virtue of what condition or disability) it is needed … the failure to distinguish various kinds of need has been disastrous for many children.* (Warnock, 2005: 20)

The 1978 Warnock Committee's second error, 'possibly the most disastrous legacy' (2005: 20), was the failure to clearly designate as SEN either children whose mother tongue was not English or those living in particularly deprived circumstances. This has led to a fudging of the links between social deprivation and learning disability which continues to this day. It has further meant that schools have found themselves having to cope with a sizeable proportion of such pupils with this double disadvantage.

Challenges in challenging circumstances

This chapter has attempted to portray something of the relationships between schools and communities and the policy which impact on their futures. We have argued that improvement strategies need to be located within the broader policy impetus, directed towards regenerating neighbourhoods, which in turn rely on not only significantly increased levels of funding but radical rethinking of what education is for as well as how and where it is provided.

For schools in challenging circumstances more sources of funding have, in fact, been made available over the last decade but they can often be no more than temporary palliatives. The Single Regeneration Budget (initiated in 1994) and Neighbourhood Renewal Funds as well as funding from the European Union through its European Regional Development Fund are, however, an explicit acknowledgement that housing, health and employment are the infrastructural trilogy of educational opportunity. While there are signs of changed thinking, progress is slow.

We may be accused of having painted too bleak a picture, particularly in light of the extraordinary things in inner-city classrooms which lighten up even the most depressing of urban landscapes. We argue, however, that it is only when policy makers are prepared to grapple with the multiple dimensions of disadvantage, and the discourse which frames it, that we can truly understand the nature, limits and potential of improvement for schools on the edge.

QUESTIONS FOR REFLECTION AND DISCUSSION

1. How helpful is 'social capital' in explaining the challenges faced by schools on the edge?
2. How does the concept of social capital apply to the school as an organisation?
3. What factors in school and community contribute to the evidence of continuing disadvantage and discrimination against certain ethnic groups? In what ways might these factors play out differently in schools on the edge?
4. With reference to providing for children with special needs, what would need to be done to ensure that 'the law of natural distribution' was observed on a national basis?

4

Schools of Hope

In 2000 eight schools were chosen by the DfES to be part of a bold initiative designed to show that, even in the most challenging of neighbourhoods, schools could improve dramatically. This chapter provides glimpses into the schools as they were before the DfES intervention, set against the background of their troubled communities. It suggests:

- they were chosen because there were so many good things already happening and because they were fertile ground in which to grow exemplary practice;
- although serving communities where hope had sometimes died, these eight schools themselves were places of hope for a better future.

Introducing eight schools

Eight schools were chosen by the DfES in 2000 to take part in a project which would demonstrate that, with the right kind of support and challenge, even schools on the edge could turn failure to success. These eight schools were not the 'worst' in the country, although the press often liked to portray them in that light, but chosen as a 'sample', representative of many other schools facing exceptionally challenging circumstances. One of the distinguishing features of this 'Octet', as they came to be known, was that they had not resigned themselves to a hopeless future. They were judged to be schools that with visionary leadership could be turned round, offering wider lessons that could be learned about improvement, even in the most apparently hopeless of places.

In selecting these eight secondary schools to take part in the project the DfES applied four key criteria. These were: 15% or fewer of the students achieving

5+ A* to C grades in 1999 and 2000; 40% or more of the students eligible for free school meals; 39% or more on the special education needs register; and good or better leadership as reported in their most recent Section 10 inspection by Ofsted. All of these eight schools had a legacy of underachievement which stretched back to 1994. Attainment at KS4, in terms of the percentage of students gaining 5 A*–Cs at GCSE/GNVQ, has varied year to year from 1% to 21%. However for most of the schools for most of the period between 1994 and 2001, it had not risen above 15% (DfES performance statistics).

The eight chosen schools were Campion in Liverpool, The Channel School in Folkestone, Havelock School in Grimsby, Pennywell in Sunderland, Phoenix School in Hammersmith and Fulham (London), St Albans CE School in Birmingham, The Ridings School in Halifax, and Whitefield School in Barnet (London). While sharing common indices of disadvantage these eight schools were, in many respects, quite different. They ranged in size from just over 400 students to almost 1,200. They included two faith schools and one single sex school. In 2001, three of the schools had some form of post-16 provision while five did not. Four are located in local authorities with grammar schools cheek by jowl with 'comprehensives', while others compete with comprehensive schools employing less overt selection policies. Five of the schools are located in mono-ethnic white wards and serve very local communities from which almost all of their students are drawn. By contrast, three others draw from scattered and highly transient multi-ethnic communities, involving young people in long and time consuming journeys to and from school.

On the wrong side of competition

A consistent theme which unites these eight schools is their 'undesirability' in the eyes of local residents, who tend to opt wherever possible either for selective schools, faith schools or schools in 'better' communities. In a competitive environment all of these schools have lost prospective students to other more 'attractive' schools. This means that school staff have been obliged to devote considerable energy to attracting students while at the same time trying to recruit teachers to what are seen as undesirable areas. All have suffered because of the breach of principles of fairness and equity in the schools with whom they are obliged to compete. In Chapter 3 we quoted the headteacher who described this as 'the name of the game', as if he were resigned to the inevitability of rules being rigged in favour of his competitors. The unequal competition does, however, have profound effects not only on the social mix but on the parent constituency, draining off the most informed and ambitious of parents.

The differences among these eight schools are just as striking and significant as the common features which bring them together. Their surface similarities conceal deeper lying differences which belie attempts by policy makers to treat them as suffering from the same malaise and prescribing a common remedy. The communities they serve are widely separated geographically and with varied histories, and the physical locations in which these schools sit do not always reflect the neighbourhoods they serve. A mapping of the primary schools on which they draw tells the story of policy initiatives, a push and pull of market forces, active and informed parental choice on the one hand and, on the other, passive resignation to the inevitable.

Eight communities on the edge

Two of the eight schools, Whitefield and Phoenix, are in London. Although geographically in the same city, they are separated culturally by the very different constituencies which they serve. On the Indices of Deprivation (ODPM, 2004) where 1= most deprived, Barnet, where Whitefield is located, was ranked at 193 out of 354 local authorities in England while Hammersmith and Fulham, home to Phoenix, was ranked at 65.

Barnet is on the outer edge of London boroughs comprising a mosaic of different wards – to the north middle class suburbs and to the south high density housing and a large minority ethnic population. The academic profile for the borough as a whole conceals the dichotomy between three very high performing grammar schools and some of the lowest performing schools in the country. Whitefield (a mixed 11–18 comprehensive with 802 pupils on roll in 2001) was described by staff as a 'dumping ground' for challenging students, pushed out of other neighbouring boroughs. This is combined with a high turnover due to immigration and re-housing, so that by Year 11 only a minority of students had been in the school since Year 7. At the beginning of the SFECC initiative the school took students from up to 70 widely scattered feeder primaries, with a gender imbalance skewed towards boys, in part due to its status as a specialist sports college.

Like Barnet, Hammersmith and Fulham is a patchwork of affluent as well as deprived neighbourhoods with ethnic minorities clustered within a few wards, so that although three quarters of the population is white, the area in which Phoenix is located has a quite distinctive ethnic profile representing over 50 nationalities. Sitting on the fringe of the vibrant community of Shepherd's Bush, its most immediate neighbour is the monolithic and troubled White City council estate. In the view of local youth workers the term 'community' is a misnomer as the area is one of volatile 'pockets' whose residents never remain long enough to develop a neighbourhood identity. In 2003, 104 of Phoenix's 750 students were refugees, primarily from Somalia, 113 from travelling families, while four out of five students were from lone parent families. The school takes students from at least nine local primary schools, most of which only send a small proportion of their students to Phoenix, parents in the main opting for schools further afield and in neighbouring boroughs.

Two of the other schools are located in major cities, St Albans in Birmingham and Campion in Liverpool. Both cities exemplify great industrial centres, repositioning themselves as cultural magnets for the twenty-first century. Birmingham is a city located in the very centre of the country, a transport hub serving a thriving industry. While three quarters of its population is estimated to live in the least deprived areas of the country, it also has its share of highly disadvantaged communities. In nine Birmingham wards, 75% of the population falls within the 10% of the most deprived residents in England. The ward in which St Albans is situated is multi-ethnic, with 78% at the latest census from minority groups, in part due to it being an area of first settlement for successive waves of refugees. Tower blocks, built in the 1960s and largely abandoned by long-term tenants, now provide short-term housing for asylum seekers and people moved out of institutional care. St Albans, a small voluntary-aided Church of England 11–16 school, with around 416 students on roll in 2001, draws its students from as many as 30 feeder primary schools, the closest primary school sending only 20% of its students to the school, the rest to several alternative secondary schools at least a bus ride away. The impact of the transient nature of the neighbourhoods it serves is expressed in a 30% turnover of students year on year.

Like Birmingham, Liverpool is experiencing an economic upturn with major regeneration projects, inward business investment and an increase in jobs for local people. The city has been awarded the title of European Capital of Culture 2008 and more recently status as a UNESCO World Heritage Site. Nonetheless, Liverpool as a whole is ranked as one of the most (if not the most) deprived local authority areas in the country. The school serves the three poorest wards in North Liverpool where only three in ten adults are in work, some 40% have no educational qualifications and 15% of all adults are long-term sick or disabled. Of the 600 or so pupils on roll in 2001, 95% were white mono-ethnic and all were boys. This, staff feel, carries its own particular stigma as unemployment and higher than average crime levels in tandem with public perceptions, impact more acutely on young men.

Sunderland and Halifax (homes to Pennywell School and The Ridings School respectively) are both cities coming to terms with a post-industrial future. In Sunderland deprivation is broadly based and affects the whole of the city. Lack of jobs and available housing in 'nice environments' has caused an outward migration of high earners from the city to other areas, while the city cannot meet the demand for re-housing for the high percentage of the population reliant on welfare benefits as their sole income. Sunderland is 15th out of 354 authorities in the government's index of multiple deprivation and 11 out of 25 wards, including the ward in which Pennywell is located (an 11–16 school, with just under 1,200 pupils on roll in 2001) are among the top 10% most deprived in the country. The Pennywell estate is marked by vandalised and boarded-up houses, with 400 empty and a further 800 due for demolition, one or two providing a temporary home for asylum seekers who experience racist abuse due to the ward being 99% white mono-ethnic. In the area closest to Pennywell School, at the start of the project up to half the adults had been unemployed over the preceding 12 months. While the student turnover is not high compared with other Octet schools, many of its student population have been excluded from other schools or are, in the words of a staff member, 'looking to escape from their previous backgrounds'.

The local constituencies of North Halifax, where the Ridings School is located, sit in stark contrast to the ethnic diversity of West Central Halifax. The area where. The Ridings is located has residents who are mainly white Protestant. It is noted for its local support of the far-right British National Party. Local housing betrays a history of neglect. The Jumbles block of flats, which lay empty for over 15 years was finally being condemned and razed to the ground, while Abbey Park, an award winning development in the 1960s, was demolished in the late 1990s as the houses were unfit to live in. The Ridings (a mixed 11–18 mixed comprehensive with some 680 pupils on roll in 2001) has a number of feeder primary schools several of whom send a significant number of students to two local faith schools close by. Many of the local Asian families prefer to send their children to a more distant alternative, The Halifax High School. Competition also comes from North Halifax Grammar School, which creams off the top 10% of the ability range in North Halifax.

Folkestone and Grimsby (homes to Channel School and Havelock School) were both once thriving seaports now in decline, Grimsby bypassed by the progressive loss of the fishing industry and Folkestone now bypassed by the Channel tunnel. Problems faced by coastal towns are compounded by unique barriers to economic development attributable to their peripherality, restricted local markets and lack of economies of scale. Folkestone sits on the very edge of the country and looks across a narrow stretch of water to France, which can be seen on a clear day. Travellers who used to pass through on their way to the ferry, unaware of the backwaters of the town which hide unemployment and poverty, described it as one of the worst in the country (Parliamentary Select Committee, 2006). The fishing, tourism and ferry industries are continuing to experience long-term contraction, bringing social and economic deprivation and environmental degradation. Kent's coastal towns have for a long time become home to large numbers of 'looked after' children (many from outside the county), as well as benefit claimants and people discharged from mental health institutions. The population of Shepway district where the Channel School is located (a mixed 11–16 school with 780 pupils on the roll in 2001) is 97% mono-ethnic with one in five residents suffering long term illness, while in the school itself 67% of students are on the register of special needs. These young people come from seven local primary schools, with much higher proportions of students from these schools opting for its main local competitor as well as sending their 'brightest' students to local grammar schools.

Grimsby too is a seaside town but with none of the attractions to merit that depiction. It is described as on the 'road to nowhere' (http://en.wikipedia.org/wiki) as it sits on the eastern eastern edge of the country and faces out to the North Sea where most of its revenue came from in more prosperous times. Together with Immingham it remains the largest port in the UK, but has suffered particularly badly from the decline of the fishing industry and the closure in 2005 of the Bird's Eye frozen fish factory, which for generations had been the main source of employment for the town. Grimsby is ranked 67th out of 354 local authorities in England on the deprivation index, marked by low grade housing, levels of unemployment at twice the national average as well as high levels of drugs, burglary and domestic violence. Havelock School, a mixed 11–16 school with just under 700 pupils on roll in 2001, is on the outskirts of the town, drawing its students mainly from the white mono-ethnic ward of Heneage (98% white), and fed by three main primary schools plus two others which send a small proportion of their students to Havelock. The headteacher comments that many of the students were of low birth weight, are under-nourished, physically small and underweight for their age, contributing to a high incidence of absence and illness.

CASE STUDY

Life before SFECC: Havelock School

Havelock School is sited on the edge of its catchment area, the old fishing community of Grimsby, a mono-ethnic ward described as one of the most deprived in the country. The poor physical state of the school buildings did not help the challenge of reaching out to parents, and the headteacher Jane Dyer put considerable effort into raising additional finance to upgrade the school environment.

At the beginning of the 1980s there were over 1,200 students at the school, including a thriving sixth form. School reorganisation in 1990 resulted in all Grimsby schools losing their sixth form, and parents increasingly sent their children to other schools in nearby Cleethorpes. Havelock's roll fell to 494, and the local authority wanted to close the school.

(Continued)

(Continued)

Damaging headlines did not help the school's cause. The school counteracted this by getting upbeat pictures of children into newspapers as it had learned that the main thing that leads to increased numbers is word of mouth in the community. Staff worked hard at attracting prospective parents, with open evenings planned to take place earlier in the year than other schools, and transport provided for parents as a further incentive. Large numbers of parents now attend open evenings, as well as parents of children already at the school regularly attending presentations evenings for attainment, effort and personal achievements. This, along with the practice of sending home commendations from both heads of department and pastoral heads, has added to the positive 'word on the street'. Staff have also worked very hard at making links and marketing Havelock, visiting primary schools in its pyramid and giving people tours of the school. The external work has been underpinned by the internal hard graft of improving teaching and learning.

The school has its own education welfare officer as well as a child support assistant who works on liaison and attendance. A senior youth worker, originally funded by the EAZ and SRB, works two days a week in the school providing counselling for youngsters with behavioural difficulties, and is available for informal lunch time discussion. The pastoral system is a strength of the school, which may have contributed to the attraction of a disproportionate number of pupils with SEN and students excluded from other schools, since the school has a good reputation for supporting them. However, this has had the effect of skewing Havelock's overall pupil profile with a consequent impact on the school's performance and position in 'league' tables. As two academies are planned to be opened locally in 2008, Havelock will be 'remodelled' as an 11–16 school.

Differences in common

While the local character of these communities defies attempts to define common features, their common challenges are captured by some or all of the indicators of economic and social disenfranchisement and by the lack of social capital. Communities in parts of these eight towns and cities are characterised by insularity and disillusionment as their work-based identity has been progressively eroded. Areas in all of these towns and cities are also home to highly transient populations, including people drawn to the casual work and the twilight economies of major urban centres. Among their numbers are asylum seekers and refugees in temporary accommodation while others are leaving troubled domestic and social situations behind. 'Family life' rarely fits the image that such a phrase might conjure up.

In many of these communities a stable core of long-term residents lives side by side with a population constantly on the move, flowing in and out of the neighbourhood in response to the pressures of immigration, housing and the job market. At the same time there are generations of families who have succeeded generations before them, with many young people who have never ventured beyond the locality in which they were born. Without local employment opportunities or leisure facilities in the neighbourhood, the school is typically one of the only places for evening, weekend and summer activities such as sports clubs, computer classes or adult education classes. In both these highly transient and more settled populations there are families and young people who slip through the net of social and community services. For them, the school is one of the few social centres which can provide a range of care and support or put families in touch with welfare services.

The term 'community' may be too romantic a concept to describe many of these neighbourhoods. The 'community' may be just a temporary stop for some whilst those who remain longterm are either tethered to their area by history or trapped by lack of mobility or economic opportunity. The 'left behind' are in estates with boarded up and firebombed houses or flats owned by private landlords, offering little in the way of aspirational housing to young people. Furthermore, in some areas, the character of the local population can shift rapidly and continuously in terms of its mix of background, ethnicities and cultures.

CASE STUDY

Life before SFECC: St Albans CE School

St Albans School is in Birmingham's Highgate, an area described as being without a strong sense of identity, a refuge for the downwardly mobile and the casualties of society. Problems, according to the local youth worker, have been largely to do with misspending – £7.7 million in SRB of which £6.6 million was spent on upgrading the three tower blocks.

There is little in the way of safe social leisure facilities for the local community. Clubs and local pubs have an increasingly bad reputation for guns or drugs, one pub having lost its licence because of drug dealing. According to the community workers, there is open crack dealing in an alley out of sight of the CCTV.

(Continued)

(Continued)

The school itself, built in the 1960s, sits on a small and cramped site. It is showing its age and crying out for radical refurbishment. It lacks sports and playing facilities, though there are plans to extend these. The student population represents 37 different first languages. More than 80 per cent of its students are classified as SEN.

The school has a loyal and supportive staff who like working in the school and share a strong collegial sense. Support staff are very often people local to the area or parents of students so have that extra commitment to their work. There are young staff in roles of responsibility for which they have been trained in the school, although it is also inevitable that such young, good leaders then sometimes move on to a bigger school. The school encourages the students in their faith and there is an ethos of respecting the individual. The students are largely polite, pleasant, friendly and well-behaved and there are fewer behaviour or attitude problems. This is largely due to the very considerable investment of time, resources and personnel who provide pastoral care and the supportive work of learning mentors and counsellors. The 1999 Ofsted report praised the dedication of the staff and the effective leadership in the school but voiced concerns about the low attainment at KS4, the lack of language support and the lack of vocational courses at KS4. In 2000 a quarter of the student body left school without any qualifications while the school had an absence rate of 17 per cent.

The exceptional challenges St Albans faces are not likely to go away in a foreseeable future – fragmentation of the communities which serve the school, tensions and volatility in young people's lives which undermine the best attempts at planning and sustainability (Ofsted, 1999).

Schools have got used to the idea that they must compete for students and, for those on the edge, the fact that they will probably end up on the wrong side of any comparisons. Interestingly Phoenix featured on the 'wrong' side of a contrast presented by entrepreneur and philanthropist Sir Peter Lampl (2004) to illustrate how some schools are left on the edge by virtue of the push and pull of market policies. At Phoenix one in seven students in 2004 were refugee children, only one in four achieving an A* to C grade pass at GCSE. Three miles away at the highly oversubscribed but 'non selective' London Oratory School (to which the Blair family sent their eldest son), 96% achieved A* to C passes. In Phoenix over half of all students were eligible for free school meals while at the Oratory the figure was just 8%. In Phoenix over 40% had some form of special educational need as compared with 10% at the London Oratory. Sharpening his point Sir Peter concluded:

> In social mobility we have gone into reverse ... I don't think there is one child at the Phoenix School who would dream of applying to the Oratory and I don't think there is one child at the Oratory who would ever go to Phoenix. So although the schools are in the same area you have perfect segmentation.

Policy makers tend to assume that schools will be adept at developing a coherent school–community strategy, and specifically a school–local business strategy. Such assumptions are challenged in a report for the Joseph Rowntree Foundation by Crowther et al. (2003) which points out that while individual headteachers may possess such expertise, entrepreneurial skill cannot be taken as a given. Given pressures on schools to improve performance statistics year on year, constantly on the lookout to recruit the best staff, appeal to the most motivated parents and attract the most promising students, competition and collaboration are uneasy bedfellows. This is not to suggest that schools, such as those represented by the Octet, do not have a niche in the market place. Unfortunately, it is one which places them on the wrong side of the improvement equation.

In all eight schools the student body contained a disproportionately high number of students with special learning needs ranging from between 40 and 60% at the outset of the project. This social and academic mix not only impacts powerfully on the internal dynamic of the school but also affects perceptions and expectations in the local community. In the Channel School, for example, staff described the negative effects of being well known for dealing with students with autism and Asperger's syndrome. At Campion in Liverpool, similarly disadvantaged by perception and prejudice, the school wanted to change its intake but was dissuaded by a local authority which was basically 'satisfied' with Campion's current role.

The challenge of adverse social circumstances is to try and compete not only on an uneven playing field but with players who do not understand the rules of the game. The goals to be reached are the same as elsewhere but in a situation where little can be taken for granted and the future is always uncertain.

Reaching out to parents

Though we have no direct evidence of the literacy levels of parents in these schools, there is a high proportion of local families in both static and transient communities with no academic qualifications. It may be inferred in both cases that traditional written forms of communication are going to be less effective than in other communities (an NFER survey for the SFECC project managers produced only a 7% return). Written forms of communication between home and school are often hazardous, so that newsletters, circular letters, report cards, forms to be filled in and returned may never reach their destination, especially when entrusted to the schoolbag mail. There is, therefore, much greater reliance on spoken face-to-face interaction, but this not only demands considerable time and effort but is subject to disruption and unanticipated crises. Low attendance at parents' meetings is explained by domestic and financial pressures, travel, prior negative experiences of school and lack of confidence in dealing with professionals.

CASE STUDY

Life before SFECC: Campion School

The school building – a '60s style, flat-roofed, rectangular-box – and its black bitumen playground is surrounded by an intimidating industrial-scale spiked metal barrier fence. New-build red brick and tile two storey residential accommodation, organised on a pattern of closes, is a feature of the local environment. These sit alongside 1950s/60s high density housing, the legacy of mixed residential and industrial layout of the area evidenced by the many blocked-off or railed-off side roads that once provided access to and from warehouses, small factories and pubs. Drug use figures high on the list of endemic local problems.

Campion was originally formed out of the merger of two Catholic secondary modern schools and a bilateral school. Since performance tables were first published, Campion has been 'bottom of the pile' in terms of the national averages for grades A to C in the headline subjects of English, maths and science. More than 60 per cent of pupils are eligible for free school meals.

Despite its bleak location Campion staff feel they have a unique and extremely positive ethos of professional and collegial support. They have a high level of commitment to one another and a pride in being 'inner-city teachers'. Several members of staff were described as having 'given their lives to these kids' and LEA inspectors praised the high quality of on-site care extended to the boys. The headteacher Tony Phillips sees the school's key function as 'operating on the very frontline in the struggle to create a culture of expectation, aspiration and optimism'.

(Continued)

(Continued)

The school has pursued a policy of celebrating student success whether in sport, commerce, community orientated activity or employment, and of building positive relationships with parents. It has a dedicated Parents' Centre, staffed by a qualified teacher, and functions to support family literacy and family numeracy through courses and qualifications (for example, a computer 'driving licence') inducting parents into the idea of 'lifelong learning' while simultaneously seeking to build parent–school relationships. The school continues to pursue an ongoing and productive relationship with Liverpool Hope University College, where a number of former Campion students are studying for, or have gained, first degrees, and Hope University undergraduates act as mentors to Campion students. Another longstanding project involves the training of selected Campion students in maritime skills, linked to guaranteed employment for boys successfully completing this programme.

The challenges for the future crystallise around the short-termist and low aspirational 'culture' and the constant struggle to engage young people in a curriculum that seems to have little to offer them.

School staff attest to the importance, but attendant frustrations, of trying to arrange face-to-face meetings with parents as well as dealing with the confrontations provoked by misunderstanding, rumour, miscommunication and treatment of their children perceived by parents as unfair or discriminatory. On the other hand, parents may see teaching or pastoral staff as a source of advice or counseling and place extra pressures on already overstretched staff. One head described parents coming to the school with issues and problems in preference to contacting official agencies such as social work or the police.

In families where English is not the first language, communication becomes still more complicated. While the students themselves are often used as a translation resource by their families, this is not always appropriate (for example when the student is in trouble) and among certain ethnic groups can upset the balance of authority within a family. Given the sheer number of first languages spoken in homes, translation services can be an important community resource and a useful conduit between the school and the community. For example, some new ethnic groups, such as a group of Somalian parents in the Highgate area served by St Albans School, often bring their own adult translator with them.

The significance of links with parents and local community predates the initiation of the SFECC project and all of the eight schools were already attempting to reach out to parents in different ways. Several of the Octet schools, designated community schools, offered adult vocational courses out of school hours. Some had facilities shared by the community. Campion School and St Albans have dedicated family centres open during school hours as well as after school and they are staffed on a full-time basis.

Links with primary schools

As Octet schools must compete for their students, how they are perceived by potential feeder primary schools has been a critical influence on their attempts to raise and maintain standards. Patterns of transition from primary to secondary schools have weighed heavily against them. Their ability to engage with the community around them depends to a large extent on geography, transport networks, the location of competing schools and, most significantly, the legacy of the past and the inertia of local tradition. For example, the primary school which sits on the doorstep of Phoenix High School sent only ten of their pupils to them out of a possible cohort of sixty. This was in part because of a turbulent historic legacy, in part because Phoenix children leave school at 3.30 p.m. when misbehaviour is highly visible to local residents. Often it is not Phoenix students themselves who are poorly behaved but as the school empties it attracts significant numbers of local youths whose misbehaviour is interpreted by residents as a 'Phoenix problem'. Hence very concerted efforts have to be made to bring in potential parents to show them the range of activities that Phoenix can offer. At Havelock in Grimsby the same issue expresses itself quite differently. Young people who live nearby nevertheless choose to go to another secondary school situated close to the primary schools they attended and which is closer to the centre of town. After school clubs in Havelock are an initiative designed to attract and retain more local students but are viewed as out of the way and on the edge of town. Even a school with a largely local student population, however, such as Campion in Liverpool, has to deal with the paradox of parents who, by virtue of real first-hand of knowledge of the school, fall back on their own perceptions or prejudices and send their children elsewhere.

The Ridings maintains close contact with its nearest primary school and the two schools share the same vice-chairman of governors. The head was invited to meet the Ofsted team during an inspection and students from the two schools share joint Culture Club activities. At Whitefield in north London teachers (including members of the SEN Department, the new Year 7 Team and the EAL Department) visit every incoming Year 6 student in their primary school and collect detailed information on every child. For both schools, the investment of time and effort involved in maintaining and developing these links is immense (given, for example, the 70 feeder primary schools which Whitefield draws from). These schools have long recognised that parents matter and that it is primarily through forging better, closer, more ongoing links with families that schools will be able to build the social capital which, as one head put it, is 'out there'.

CASE STUDY

Life before SFECC: Phoenix School

Phoenix School rose from the ashes of Hammersmith School, a fresh start under a new headteacher but still with the legacy of a deeply troubled school, characterised by the *Mail on Sunday* as the worst school in Britain with out-of-control students, rock-bottom staff morale and open drug dealing.

In 2000 the recruitment and retention crisis was hitting Phoenix hard with 30 per cent understaffing. Temporary staff filled only a short-term gap, adjusting slowly and often painfully to the local culture, requiring immense support, then moving on again just when they had found their feet. In 2001 Ofsted acknowledged the difficulties as lying beyond the school and to a large extent outside its control, while praising the 'dynamic leadership' of the headteacher William Atkinson in 'trying to raise standards in difficult circumstances'. Concerted efforts were made to target underachievement, to challenge self belief, to raise expectations and put in place incentives, tangible rewards for achievement, and public celebration of success.

Special grants, Excellence in Cities and the Neighbourhood Regeneration Grant were used to fund a wide range of after-school activities, including adult education, family learning and a Youth Link intervention project with courses on anger management and dealing with crime, among many others. Teaching staff were complemented by a family support social worker, a speech and language therapist, a nurse, a primary liaison teacher, a literacy programme co-ordinator, a student counsellor, a parent and family support worker, a teenage pregnancy worker and learning mentors. A member of staff worked with Black British (Caribbean) young people at risk of exclusion.

Before SFECC 'the school was not a desert' says the headteacher, pointing to a wide range of initiatives such as Master Classes for gifted and talented students; artists in residence; visiting dance, jazz and drama groups; a part-time professional disc jockey; African and Indian dance, rock and hip hop schools; gospel choir; African drumming, mime

(Continued)

(Continued)

and mask making; video and sound editing in the school's own studio and projects with the BBC; coaching skills at Queens Park Rangers; and numerous programmes with police on safety, drugs, car crime and neighbourhood involvement.

Imagination, invention and hard work by staff with tremendous pride in the school has not been repaid in full because of the continued challenges of recruiting and retaining high quality teachers, and the energy required to compete on an increasingly uneven playing field.

The power of image

In an age of instant and transient media image making, the Octet schools have had to work hard at constructing alternative versions of what they are. Some even became 'causes célèbres' by virtue of incessant and high profile media coverage. However, negative perceptions of schools, in part derived from Performance Tables (especially at a time when performance statistics did not include any notion of 'value-added'), and in part from local 'intelligence', combined to make SFECC schools less attractive than their more favoured competitors. The stigma attached to a 'failing' school or a school requiring Special Measures compounded the demoralising effect on staff and students. Nor has the public image of these schools been helped by a proportion of the school's intake being 'over-age' students, refugees, new arrivals or casual admissions.

CASE STUDY

Life before SFECC: The Ridings School

Most of the young people who come to The Ridings live in post-war social housing built as a result of town-centre slum clearances. The Programme Director of North Halifax SRB partnership comments that these tightly packed housing estates represent 'a concentration of deprivation squeezed into very dense housing where parental unrest spreads like wildfire from house to house'.

(Continued)

(Continued)

In November 1996, The Ridings was placed in Special Measures with devastating effect on the morale of staff and students, exacerbated by shrill and dramatic press coverage which, said staff, 'totally undermine the whole community'. ABC from the USA camped on the pavements outside the school for two days, with lurid reports of the first 'Failing School' in England.

When the school came out of Special Measures in October 1998 staff commented on feelings of 'optimism and vindication', 'jubilation', 'a mixture of elation, great relief, pride and tiredness' as the 'the stigma has been lifted'. Extensive efforts were undertaken to raise self-esteem. Progress was slow and hard won. Teachers as well as students needed huge amounts of praise and reinforcement: 'one step back for every two forward'.

In 2001 the Ofsted inspection declared this 'a good and improving school', and in July of that year the school had its best Key Stage 3 results ever. Improvement was ascribed to the appointment of Anna White as headteacher in addition to a significant number of senior leaders in 1998; a collegiate approach to leadership; constant praise and reinforcement for teachers as well as students; the capital investment that followed being placed in Special Measures; complementing the 'academic' curriculum with a vocational curriculum; committed and enthusiastic staff including 30 teaching support assistants and a supportive senior management.

However external factors continued to push against internal improvement: the creaming off by two faith schools and a grammar school; the significant number of pupils with EBD needs who still make up the majority of pupils; the lack of viable LEA alternative provision for severely emotionally and behaviourally disturbed young people; accountability demands; continual casual admissions every year; the depressed local economy, poverty, poor housing and unemployment; the insularity of the town; and perhaps most critically the high turnover of staff, up to one third in 2002–03, leaving key posts unfilled.

'Success in this environment is a very fragile thing' it was said then and so it proved as, following the Ofsted inspection in 2005, the school was given 'notice to improve ... in relation to: standards and provision in the sixth form; achievement and progress of pupils; attendance and behaviour; the quality of provision of teaching and of the curriculum'.

Coping with turbulence: the effects of staff and student mobility

When the SFECC project began, some of the schools were in a period of transition. New headteachers were still finding their feet and were recovering from Special Measures. Many of the Octet schools were suffering acutely from the movement of staff in and out of the school as the project began. As one headteacher put it:

> *The biggest pressure at the moment is that of getting and keeping staff. Vacancies sometimes get no applicants ... but management structures and evaluation structures are of little use if you haven't got living, breathing, exciting people in front of youngsters. Good teachers are the key to it all.*

CASE STUDY

Life before SFECC: The Channel School

The Channel School is located on a small industrial estate in the coastal town of Folkestone. It had long suffered from being the school of last resort in a system which still operated 11 plus selection. This meant that it always had more than its fair share of the most troubled children, but more recently had begun to take in a large number of asylum seekers' children. It has always been a largely white population (96 per cent according to the 1999 Ofsted report) and was notorious for violent classroom invasions by National Front activists in the late 1970s.

In 1996 the school came out of its first episode of Special Measures and in the following two years there were signs that the turbulence of the early 1990s had been overcome. By 1999 the signs were very positive. The school was awarded £150,000 from the Single Regeneration Budget which enabled the appointment of a Community Development Manager and later a Business Links Manager, as well as the provision of mentoring, signalling a desire to focus on work related and vocational learning.

In the years leading up to the SFECC project, Channel School had enjoyed a period of stability with signs that pointed to the possibility of improvement. The 1999 Ofsted Report indicated that the school was on the mend and might be able to overcome the extremely challenging

(Continued)

(Continued)

circumstances it faced. The school had benefited from the established leadership of a mature, caring team who had been responsible for leading the school out of 'Special Measures'. The invitation to join the SFECC/Octet project towards the end of 2000 seemed to reinforce the idea that the school was continuing its climb out of difficulty.

However, January of 2001 saw a significant faltering of progress. A fire destroyed part of the school and standards of pupil behaviour were said to have deteriorated. Levels of teacher stress were high and a large number of teachers left the school at the end of the 2000–2001 academic year. In September 2001 at the start of the SFECC project the school was in worse circumstances than those reported by Ofsted two years earlier. The percentage of students achieving 5 A*–C grades at GCSE was 9 per cent in 2001, a consequence of large numbers of temporary teaching staff and poor standards of behaviour. The headteacher's health became a problem at this time, leading to long-term absence and eventual retirement, and until 2003 the school was led by an acting-up deputy. In 2003 a new head, Collette Singleton was appointed to take the school into a new era and in 2004 the school was again taken out of Special Measures.

By 2005 when the SFECC project ended, Kent County Council had given the go ahead for the school to be closed and re-opened as the new Folkestone Academy.

The unsettling effect of understaffing and continuous turnover was to continue during the three years of the project. There were significant shortages and constant changes in senior leadership teams. During the first year, when systems and structures were being put into place, three heads retired, two of them through ill-health. The Channel School had three acting heads in the first 18 months of the project and only in January 2003 was a full-time headteacher appointed. At Pennywell, a new head began almost one year into the project. By the beginning of the autumn term of the school year 2002–2003, when the 'implementation stage' of the project began, Campion was without a full-time head. The previous head had retired and his proposed replacement, then the deputy head, was precipitously relieved of his job. The retiring head was then prevailed upon to return to cover for the post until a permanent replacement could be found, something that did not occur until later in the school year. There was similar significant turnover of other members of the senior leadership team. Pennywell was without a deputy head for 2003–2004, while the head of the Humanities Department was simultaneously running the Science department. At The Ridings School, there was a vacancy for a deputy head in September 2003, a post that had still not been filled a year later. One of the assistant heads at St Albans was on long-term sick leave during 2003–2004 and had not returned to the school by the time the project ended.

In addition to these staffing crises, three of the schools were also experiencing extreme mobility of students at the outset of the project. Situations where up to half the cohort could change between Year 7 and Year 11, made tracking of students' progress difficult. The fragmentation of learning was also apparent in the number of students leaving Year 11 with no GCSE qualifications.

Heroic leadership in challenging circumstances

One of the criteria in the selection of schools for the project was the 'quality of leadership', couched specifically in terms of heads with the capacity to turn schools round, allied to providing relevant support and professional development. Much expectation rested on the shoulders of heads, and much of the focus of the SFECC intervention was targeted on them. These were eight very different people with differing profiles of experience, differing leadership styles and beliefs about what defines leadership and how it expresses itself in the day-to-day life of the school. Apart from their common commitment to their schools, no simple list of qualities or competencies would be adequate to describe them. They brought widely varying experiences of headship. Two of the heads already had a high national profile and had taken over schools in the mid 1990s amid the glare of television and newspaper publicity. Two had been newly appointed from other schools. Three had been promoted within their schools and so had no previous experience of headship, while one at was appointed halfway through the project. Five were men and three were women.

In leadership style they ranged from the head clearly leading from the front, with a powerful and visible presence around the school, to others leading, more subtly from behind. This contrast was evident in the operation of the school improvement groups, set up at the outset of the project: one head choosing personally to chair the group, another to quite deliberately stay off it. These differences do not necessarily imply a more authoritarian or democratic approach but rather different ways of using authority. 'Strong' heads may use their influence directly and overtly or in more nuanced but no less powerful ways. One head's style was described by a member of his staff as 'a subtle way of shifting his authority' through a kind of 'automatic transference of authority' to whatever staff group he is setting up.

Some heads consciously modelled an upbeat outlook, putting on a positive face when confronted with adversity, not allowing a negativism or cynicism to seep through the staff culture, keeping their deepest doubts and their 'dark nights of despair' to their closest confidantes. Some invested considerable time and energy in talking up and selling their school, seeing image management, both internally and externally as a personal priority. The need for careful stage management was common to all, but where heads placed themselves and their staff on stage differed. Some were more inclined to script the performance of their actors while others, more open to improvisation, took greater risks with the outcome. A sense of trust and confidence in key players among the staff could be communicated by constant praise and reinforcement or more subtly by creating space as an implicit vote of confidence. The balance between internal and external relations varied too, devoting time to parents, to community agencies and public relations as opposed to paying close attention to daily management of the school. While the SFECC project brought heads out of their schools on regular occasions to share ideas and draw moral support, some were less faithful in their attendance because they gave greater priority to being in their schools. This could be read as a lack of confidence in staff, a self confidence which needs no moral support, or an expression of doubt as to the added value of the project.

For schools on the edge it is clear that leadership matters but how it is expressed and where it lies is a function of context, experience, personality, and varying degrees of belief that to give away authority is to gain it.

CASE STUDY

Life before SFECC: Whitefield School

Whitefield School, situated near Brent Cross in outer London has been described as a 'dumping ground' for 'challenging' pupils whom other schools and other local authorities have pushed out. Because it was not full, the school was required to take students who had not been successful elsewhere. At the beginning of the SFECC Project, the head's view was that the school's reputation locally was still poor, middle-class parents were reluctant to 'risk' the school, even to find out more about it. Discussions within the LEA as to possible closure simply worsened the problem. As little was done by the school to refute this rumour, it meant that its reputation declined further, with able pupils choosing to go elsewhere. The spiral downwards continued producing increasingly skewed intakes and falling rolls.

Nonetheless, the school has been praised for what it has achieved, particularly with black boys and children with special educational needs

(Continued)

(Continued)

The Oftsed report of 1999 commended the school for its safe, non-threatening and supportive environment, commenting that the school had responded 'exceptionally well to the individual needs of a very wide range of students'. It was seen to have high quality, committed staff who supported one another and gave very good pastoral support as well as keeping a focus on learning. The social and cultural development of students was described as good, under the leadership of a visionary head and a strong and effective senior management team, who with good systems and procedures had forged very good partnerships with industry and the community. The headteacher, Peter Blenkinsop, took over in 2000, having been promoted from within the SMT which enabled him to build on the work of the two previous heads with a long historical perspective on the changing circumstances of the school.

The headteacher's view is that in 2001, prior to SFECC, the school had already started to implement change but needed focusing on how these changes could be consolidated in the face of an annual turnover of one in five students (casual admissions of students new to the country and sometimes new to schooling). It proved very difficult for teachers to work with a constantly changing class and to plan lessons and schemes of work. The school has constantly been challenged to target its various initiatives to particular groups of students and to meet the diverse set of needs that its intake present. The head comments:

> The variation at that end of the spectrum is really quite large because often you are dealing with some really strange gaps in kids' understanding or abilities to process information. You are re-learning and re-doing what you once did. Differentiation is quite hard here because it's not a fixed set of groups you're differentiating for – you can't do what you did before to differentiate because it won't necessarily work.

Building success: beyond schooling

Whatever the balance of time spent by senior leaders in their schools and in the community, what becomes clear from the eight schools' stories is the need to promote education as reaching much beyond the confines of the school day. In differing degrees, all schools saw it as a priority to build bridges between in-school and out-of-school learning. This is reflected in the profiles of school staff in which teaching staff may be outnumbered by support staff: staff with a social and community remit, with a parental or family brief, with counselling and mentoring experience or with a role in liaising with primary schools or with other voluntary and welfare agencies.

Life before SFECC: Pennywell School

The view from Pennywell School is of connected blocks of council housing, built in the 1950s and 60s but now comprising a mixture of well maintained properties together with others vandalised and boarded-up. Some of these have been fire-bombed. There is no 'aspirational housing' for local residents looking to move up the ladder. This results in those who are doing well moving out of the area. The Pennywell Estate is a high crime-risk area with a permanent police post on the estate. Professional drug dealing is a major concern.

The number of asylum seekers being settled into some of the vacant houses in the area exacerbated racist tensions, and families have left the estate after suffering abuse from some of the residents. A widely held view is that an area like Pennywell can only support a tiny number of asylum seekers or refugees but that Pennywell's vacant housing is naturally targeted by government for short-term needs.

Prior to the present head coming into post one year into the SFECC project, Pennywell had had the same headteacher for 15 years, a strong and forceful character who had brought continuity and stability to the school. He had established a tradition of Pennywell as an open, creative and entrepreneurial school. He believed in the importance of offering students a range of possibilities to experience success, which was made as public, external and widespread as possible. This was demonstrated through outside competitions, theatre performances and, in 1999, the hosting of an international conference on peer support at the Stadium of Light in Sunderland. In 2001, Year 10 students won a regional final young engineering competition against the sixth form of a local public school and went to the final in London and then on to Belgium and France.

Pennywell staff have always been very active outside normal school hours. There is a breakfast club, a gifted and talented programme with residential weekends, and a literacy programme in the summer holidays in conjunction with several local primary schools to help students make the transition from KS2 to KS3. The school has maintained strong links with parents across generations, helped by a continuity of a stable core of long serving staff.

(Continued)

(Continued)

Despite their optimism and commitment, school staff point to the lack of employment opportunities and aspirational role models in the community, living off short-term funding, the unsettling effect of temporary staff, long-term staff too set in their ways, and the most vital and promising of teachers being promoted to schools elsewhere. In November 2004 Ofsted found the school to have 'serious weaknesses'.

In spite of the challenges and the lowly status of Octet schools in the performance tables, many important initiatives were already taking place in these schools when the project began. Several of the schools already had built, or were engaged in building, new facilities. For example at The Ridings School, in 1998 a new expressive arts block and science labs were opened and in January 2001 a new administration block was added. Havelock School had already begun an extensive building programme. A parent centre was already open at Campion and planning for the new music and dance studio at Pennywell was well underway, as were plans for the Family Centre at St Albans. There were also many local initiatives. St Albans, for example, was part of the Excellence in Cities initiative as well as a member of its local Education Action Zone. At Phoenix, a community state-of-the-art gymnasium and fitness centre was already planned. Whitefield had already achieved sports college status.

Some schools were running intensive reading or literacy programmes for their students and summer schools especially for incoming students. Some offered a wide range of before and after school provision for students in need, including breakfast clubs and extra ICT classes. These various initiatives were an important complement to the curriculum but still insufficient to address a knowledge diet that for many young people conspicuously failed to engage their interest. The number of students disaffected and disengaged from the curriculum on offer meant that many were leaving with no qualifications or with low grades. One of the opportunities offered by the SFECC project was to radically reappraise the curriculum in these schools. It was a promise that remained unfulfilled.

As the project began, visits were made by outside experts acting on behalf of the DfES to all of the eight schools between September and December 2001 to assess their state of readiness. The eight schools were judged to be focusing on a range of strategies to meet the challenges, including:

- strong management and systems;
- emphasis on image, ethos, appearance, openness and attractiveness of buildings;

- enhancement of the culture of caring and respect;
- concentration on behaviour and attendance;
- efforts to stabilise staffing and build on a core of very committed staff;
- focus on consistency of basic teaching and learning practices;
- some key appointments, particularly at middle and senior management.

In short, these schools were judged to be fertile ground for radical improvement. While all eight had aspirations and expectations for their students, some had, in the view of the DfES team, lost their way and needed an impetus and renewed energy. While all of these schools had experienced constant setbacks, the DfES project was founded on the belief that with external support and resourcing they could rise above their circumstances. That belief was put to the test over the following three years. Chapter 5 points to the major successes and highlights some of the efforts to reform encountered on the way.

QUESTIONS FOR REFLECTION AND DISCUSSION

1. Is competition always a stronger pull than collaboration or is it possible to reconcile these two seemingly opposing forces? What needs to happen in order to change perceptions of particular schools? Does one school's increase in local popularity entails another's decline?
2. Given the mix of common and distinct 'exceptionally challenging cirumstances' in these eight schools, to what extent is a common agenda of improvement suggested, and how much do local conditions influence change?
3. Are particular qualities of leadership needed to be a head-teacher of a school in 'challenging cirumstances'?
4. Why is stability in staffing so important for schools 'on the edge'? How are more good teachers and headteachers to be encouraged to work in such schools?

5

Can Governments Change Schools?

Chapter 4 described the eight schools of the Octet and the challenging circumstances in which they strived to compete with more privileged schools. This chapter:

- assesses the various components of the intervention;
- asks whether the clear success of some strands and failure of others undermined an overall coherence and sustainability;
- discusses whether government intervention can change schools, or whether the SFECC project was simply not the right way to go about it.

Governments and schools: a changing relationship

The relationship between governments and schools is one that has undergone fundamental change in the last two decades. In England the watershed was the direct interest taken by the Thatcher Government in the 1980s and 1990s in school performance, a legacy which the Labour Government continued with zeal, much education policy emanating directly from Downing Street and Blair's circle of advisers. In 1997, shortly following the election, the new Labour government established the Standards Task Force, an advisory body bringing university and school leaders into the DfES to discuss ways of improving education. It was designed to allow greater oversight and intervention from the centre. The SFECC project was one of the initiatives to come from that group, the 'big idea' being to introduce an innovative school improvement project to a small selection of urban schools in the most disadvantaged communities. Its purpose was to demonstrate how, even in those circumstances, schools could rise above the downward drag of deprived neighbourhoods. The programme was devised around a set of core premises.

- Every school can improve.
- Improvement is assessed in terms of enhanced pupil outcomes.
- Every individual in the school has a contribution to make.
- Start from where the school is, but set high goals.
- Help schools help themselves, but guard against dependency.
- Model good practice.
- Raise expectations of what is possible.

These were to be realised in practice through encouraging schools to work with external partners to:

- take early and firm intervention to secure effective management and leadership;
- help the school identify core issues through survey and data analysis;
- gain whole school staff commitment;
- introduce models of leadership and teaching quality;
- focus on dealing with issues in a phased manner in order to achieve a track record of success – Ofsted issues, environment, pride, attendance, etc.;
- keep an unrelenting focus on teaching and learning. (Hopkins et al., 2002)

The grand plan

The SFECC project was envisaged as 'cutting edge' and the schools were to be encouraged to develop radical solutions to the problems of educating their young people, as this extract from the 2001 Green Paper *Schools Building on Success* suggests:

> **4.60** *The pilot will include a strong emphasis on much smaller classes and more flexible approaches to the use of time. We want teachers who choose to work in these extremely challenging circumstances to have additional support and pupils to benefit from an extended learning day and weekend and holiday learning.* (DfEE, 2001a: 57–58)

Initial suggestions were radical: redefining the school year into four or five terms to give students extended schooling and, in particular, to reduce the long summer break. National Curriculum requirements were to be ignored in favour of a focus on basic skills such as literacy and numeracy in the first years of Key Stage 3. As indicated above, there were also plans for substantial reductions in class size. There was an overarching commitment to the increased use of ICT, directly for teaching and learning in the classroom (including the use of video link across the eight schools and a common website) and in streamlining the use of data in the schools. There were to be incentives and bonuses to encourage the recruitment and retention of staff. Other key innovations discussed included different roles in the school for support staff such as teaching assistants, and a suggested rethink for the senior leadership team with flexible teams and dual headship. The schools themselves were going to be strategic drivers of the project and the hope was for successes that could be translated to a broader group of schools.

The term 'action research' had been used by Michael Barber (the then head of the DfES Standards and Effectiveness Unit) and others in the DfES in setting up the project but the concept of action research, where agency would lie with the schools, was lost as the DfES took more and more control of the project. A DfES project adviser provided a strategic overview and organised a package of programmes. What became established was the idea of 'upskilling' through training senior leaders, middle managers and classroom teachers. Strategies to move outside the school and work together with local agencies never materialised. None of the eight local authorities were directly involved in the project and the model became one of centralised control and a direct relationship between each school and the DfES ('London Calling' as one headteacher put it). Perhaps the possibility of profound structural change was ruled out even before the project really began.

The project, as it developed on the ground, had a number of strands:

- A focus on learning with, in particular, the introduction of a reading programme to improve literacy in KS3.
- A focus on pedagogy, in particular pedagogy underpinned by ICT, using interactive whiteboards and data to inform teaching strategies and track pupil progress.
- A focus on networking through video conferencing and a common website.
- A focus on leadership through the development of school improvement groups (SIGs), training for middle managers and support for headteachers through regular meetings.
- Direct funding to each school of £150,000–£200,000 each year.

During the period of the project the schools were subject to regular monitoring visits by HMI, over and above the regular Ofsted inspections for which they were scheduled.

Learning and literacy

It is widely accepted that children have difficulty in learning if they are not proficient readers. Indeed the Octet heads had identified the low literacy levels of students starting Key Stage 3 as a major obstacle to student progress. The need was poignantly illustrated by one Year 7 student who said to the research team:

When I get told to read in class I don't feel confident ... I get all shaky and scared in case people laugh at me.

The DfES's answer was to introduce 'Ruth Miskin Literacy' (RML) a highly pre-scriptive reading, spelling, vocabulary and writing programme for slow or hesitant KS3 readers. RML promises, if its tightly stipulated content, teaching protocols and structural arrangements are followed, to take children to a decoding age (as opposed to a reading comprehension age) of 12 years. The content focuses on phonemes and graphemes, and students are taught for four one-hour lessons a week in groups of between 8 and 16, in a quiet, controlled classroom environ-ment. Students with behaviour problems and specific learning difficulties are placed in even smaller groups and no student is supposed to join the programme part way through the year. Teaching protocols include students working with a partner, a 'no hands up' rule, and patterns of repetition and drills reminiscent of teaching English as a Foreign Language to beginners. At the time the project adopted RML, there was little independent evidence of its success.

Many of the trained teachers commented, often with surprise, on the success of the RML programme, both in terms of their own role and of the way that students engaged with the activities. Four of the eight schools judged RML to be highly successful, citing evidence of increased reading ages, students able to tackle much more complex tasks in mainstream classes, and marked improvement in attitude. One head of English saw RML as addressing shortcomings in the National Curriculum to assist those who, for whatever reason, were behind in reading.

The programme is teaching students to read, to learn basic decoding skills and this is something that National Curriculum does not do. It's assumed that students can already read by the time they get to Year 7 ... Secondary English teachers, for example, are not taught how to teach reading ... the National Literacy Strategy does not address reading in an intensive way.

Keys to the success of the programme, in the view of those who favoured it, were the affirming and supportive relationship between a teacher and a small group, and the skills of the individual teacher. In one school one teacher was highly successful with RML while her colleagues were not.

However, not all SFECC schools were so positive about the programme's benefits and a number of headteachers and teachers remained sceptical. Indeed some were vitriolic in their dislike of RML and its highly prescriptive approach. Critics (including HMI) observed that students resented being taken out of their normal classes and missing lessons in other subjects, and that a school's 'normal' literacy and SEN programmes were likely to be of demonstrably greater benefit in increasing reading ages. The programme's rigidity was criticised, and its content was seen as being decontextualised with little relationship to the KS3 curriculum.

The ambivalent responses to RML and claims for its success are hard to unravel, and raise questions about its key elements. Where it did raise students' literacy skills and confidence, possible contributory factors include: individual teachers' belief in the programme, the intensity of focus, high expectations, praise and reinforcement for success, small class size, the quality of relationships, the Hawthorne effect. Nationally the pendulum has swung and phonics programmes are back in political favour (Rose, 2006). Furthermore, the reported success of synthetic phonics in Clackmannanshire (Johnston and Watson, 2003) has re-ignited the debate over preferred approaches.[1] Other commentators, meanwhile, suggest that this is a 'war' between analytic and synthetic phonics which misses the essential point that there are a host of differing ways of helping children learn to read (Wyse, 2003).

Pedagogy and technology

The project schools were encouraged to develop pedagogy through technology, and interactive whiteboards were seen as offering new scope for engaging young people in their learning. The project provided funding for two interactive whiteboards in each school and one day's training. Despite this fairly minimal provision, interactive whiteboards were one of the project's more popular strands. Teachers quickly saw ways in which whiteboards could help with engaging and controlling their classes, and some schools moved rapidly to widespread adoption. In Havelock, for example, the head secured additional finance to equip every classroom with an interactive whiteboard, and in Campion 15 were installed in the space of six months. By contrast, additional interactive whiteboards were not installed at Whitefield School until much later and there was very little development in their use during the project.

In a number of schools the 'seed' of the project's one day's training was followed up through other networks and in particular through training offered by LEAs. Experts began to emerge in some schools, operating at and beyond the leading edge of contemporary practice, crossing hierarchical boundaries and grasping leadership opportunities. Soon Havelock started planning to become a centre of excellence in relation to interactive whiteboards, and within 12 months of the initial training one of the teachers at Campion School was providing training across the LEA.

Whiteboards were often cited as the catalyst for enlivening lessons with more varied, colourful and sometimes competitive activities, and for heightening students' expectations. Among the many enthusiasts at Havelock, one teacher listed eight specific benefits:

- children working interactively on the board;
- teachers modelling research using the Internet;

- the size and range of pictures and images available;
- being able to adapt images from text books, etc.;
- the accompanying resources;
- building up a bank of resources for future use;
- sharing resources within the department;
- being able to print off work if children had been away.

A group of Year 11 students was equally enthusiastic:

> *There's a lot of technology, which enables us to learn more. It's better for us. We used to have TVs but they are too small to see. Now interactive whiteboards mean everybody can see. The teacher can also save what has been written down and go back to it, so they save time, and can recap at the beginning of the next lesson. We use the whiteboards interactively in French, and for powerpoint presentations in Leisure and Tourism and in English. It makes you feel more professional and more confident so you can perform to the best of your ability because you feel like people will take notice.*

Our own observations in a range of subjects provided evidence of lessons that had been made more exciting and accessible by the use of whiteboards. Examples of creative and successful use by imaginative teachers who knew how to exploit the medium to the full followed the principles of careful planning and maximising student participation. Individual hand-held 'Activote' devices were one way of enabling every student to respond to questions or to signal misunderstanding – a development of significant relevance as assessment for learning gains higher profile in policy and practice. HMI, in their regular monitoring, also cited examples of good practice and pointed to lessons that had helped sustain pupils' concentration and enhanced understanding.

Nevertheless there were downsides. We found frustration among school staff at the limited provision of the interactive whiteboards, and evidence of their potential being missed. Some teachers were using them for traditional didactic teaching or simply deploying them as a projector screen, often leaving students passive and frustrated in the process. In order to use interactive whiteboards to full effect teachers needed knowledge, confidence, planning time and a commitment to a learner-centred approach. Where whiteboards were not embedded as another tool in the repertoire of skilled teachers, concerns were expressed by teachers and heads about their being used for their novelty value. In a couple of cases we were warned of the dangers of 'death by whiteboard'.

Pedagogy, data and learning styles

A key aim of the project was to encourage proactive use of data for planning, although the DfES' emphasis on accountability introduced a further tension. The

DfES asked project schools to supply extra data for this purpose, attainment data having to be sent to them each half term. The idea of data management linking together different systems such as lesson planning, the performance of pupil cohorts as well as individual pupils, was recognised by the schools as potentially very powerful. However, the spreadsheet specifically developed for the project had many technical failings, and this caused delay and frustration. The flawed SFECC spreadsheet led eventually to the development of a fully fledged database system called START, introduced unfortunately only after the project was completed. Had it been fully developed earlier it might have increased the use and impact of data management within the project itself. But in response schools made progress in developing their own data systems, many of which were already being implemented in collaboration with local networks.

The data that really captured the imagination and were used by a core of champions among the staff were the CAT data. The Cognitive Aptitude Test (CAT) is a diagnostic tool used to analyse the 'learning styles' of students, who are then categorised according to their preferences for verbal, non-verbal, visual and kinaesthetic approaches. In theory at least, this makes it possible for teachers to organise activities in lessons to cater for different styles. For one of the staff from Campion School the training in using CAT data had been like 'switching on a light' and every other advance in the project had followed on from there. The 'early adopters' grasped the value of these data, their helpfulness to their teaching and the positive effects on the students of mixing and matching teaching approaches. The usefulness of CAT data possibly took on a kind of folk truth; there was enthusiasm and a sense that 'it worked'. As one teacher from Pennywell School said in 2003, 'we were data rich but now it is more a case of data smart'.

Teachers who adopted more finely differentiated teaching strategies to cater for the varied learning needs reported increased interest and positive responses from their students. These teachers' reactions mirror the growing enthusiasm in schools throughout the country for teaching focused on Multiple Intelligences (MI) and learner preferences for visual, auditory, or kinaesthetic (VAK) approaches. However, there is considerable scepticism among researchers and learning theorists who have failed to find any empirical basis for claims made for a VAK approach (Coffield et al., 2004). Indeed, Howard Gardner has distanced himself from the evangelical embrace of MI, arguing that it was never intended to be used prescriptively and naively in individual profiling and differentiating instruction (Gardner, 2003). But, whatever the case, there is no denying the fact that teachers in the project schools embraced this aspect of the project. CAT testing and the discussion of learning styles were seen as a catalyst that helped teachers recognise the individuality of learners, and the blocks to learning that traditional views of intelligence and ability do not take into account. Equally importantly they provided teachers with a reason to engage in discussions within, and sometimes across, departments about the nature of learning and individual needs.

Pedagogy and networking

The practice of schools learning from one another has attracted considerable support in recent years, not least from the National College of School Leadership. At the outset of the project the DfES promoted video conferencing and a shared website as having huge potential for dialogue on pedagogy across the schools. Besides the prospect of the more usual 'talking heads' conversations amongst the SLTs, the plan was for classroom teachers to use video conferencing to exchange practice focused on interactive whiteboards. In the event things turned out quite differently.

The schools signed up for the vision, and timetabled an early afternoon finish for a weekly sharing of curriculum and practice. Each school went through the costly business of buying and setting up the equipment. At the start of the project when the video-conferencing infrastructure was being put into place, national communication development was well underway, and it was envisaged that the equipment in the schools would work through an interconnected, Internet protocol. However, what was being proposed demanded not just a national system, but one which supported optimum quality video, so that teachers could actually see each other's work via the link. Unfortunately, this was not in place even by the end of the project. Regional firewalls were preventing signals moving across networks and there were difficulties with particular regional broadband consortia providing an easy feed for video conferencing. Furthermore, the high costs of using ISDN as an alternative were seen as prohibitive. It could be argued that this was a problem beyond the control of the DfES and that any technical innovation carries the risk of failure, but the video conferencing element of the project had been heavily promoted and the schools had taken a lot of effort to install the equipment. The consensus among the schools was that all the technical aspects ought to have been sorted out before the project was started.

Running alongside the failure of video conferencing was the failure of the SFECC website. Again, as far as the schools were concerned, a major problem was the length of time it took to get this website up and running (it was not active until well into the second year of the project) and, more importantly, it did not have much on it even by the time the project ended. As with other aspects of the project, it was unclear who should take lead responsibility, for example in posting material from the schools. According to the Project Adviser it should have been the DfES, but they lacked administrators to do this kind of task. Arguably, in another kind of project where schools had a greater sense of agency and ownership they would have done it themselves, but the centralised control of the SFECC project became increasingly entrenched.

Looking to the future, the lesson is that for video conferencing to be useful for developing pedagogy the quality has to be extremely good in order to share student work and classroom practice; the equipment also needs to be easy to access and operate. Above all a clear and coherent rationale for its use is essential. The failure of video conferencing had the knock-on effect of undermining the rationale for a website. In general, it was only a small and select group of staff from the Octet who came together at professional development events. Many staff did not appear to view sharing ideas across the eight schools as a priority, and video conferencing and a project website looked more like luxuries than practical tools.

Developing and extending leadership

Two strands of the project were concerned with developing leadership in the schools. One was training to develop a School Improvement Group, and the other a training programme for subject leaders and middle managers.

The creation of a School Improvement Group (SIG) was widely seen as the most successful aspect of the SFECC project. It was not a new initiative in every school, but the project gave it further impetus. The notion of a SIG for promoting change and professional development can be traced back to the James Report (DES, 1972). At its core is the idea that effective professional learning is school-based rather than merely school-focused, and should be linked explicitly to particular development goals.

While the SIG model of improvement bears some similarity to its IQEA predecessor (Hopkins et al., 1996) it did, nonetheless, develop its own identity. Common to both models is a cadre of staff who act as evaluators of practice and promoters of change. It is a model of improvement that is neither 'bottom up' nor 'top down', but may rather be described as 'middle out' since its influence is designed to flow 'upwards' to senior leadership as well as 'down' to individual classroom level. A key characteristic of the cadre is that its members co-ordinate development activities, involving many more colleagues in the process.

SIGs ranged in size from five to nine members, typically representing a wide range of departments and varying experience, from newly qualified teachers to established senior staff. Almost all the SIGs included a member of the senior leadership team, or a SLT member had direct responsibility for co-ordinating the work of the SIG with the strategic direction of the school. However, a significant number of SIG members were young and relatively inexperienced teachers who were given an opportunity to exercise leadership. There were attempts in some schools to use SIG membership to support 'weaker' teachers, but on the whole the SIGs derived their credibility and strength from the contributions of effective, well-regarded members of staff. While democratisation of leadership should not be overstated, the impact of teacher leadership from within the SIGs proved to be a major factor in cultural change and in demonstrating the potential of wider shared leadership.

The SIG training took place on six two-day sessions over a two-year period, and involved a core group of trainers offering a series of workshops at each residential. These included topics such as effective teaching, formative assessment, data to inform teaching and learning, the emotions of learning and teaching, and the self-esteem of both teachers and students. There were also opportunities for each SIG to focus on their own school's improvement agenda.

The fact that the SIG training occurred at regular intervals over two years proved to be a powerful factor in sustaining interest and motivation, and opportunities for socialising helped forge interpersonal bonds that fostered energy and enthusiasm. The teamwork within each SIG was another key factor, drawing together staff from different departments who had previously often neither known each other well nor collaborated. A particular aspect of the training commented upon favourably by participants was the feeding back and discussion of experiences. As one SIG member from Campion School said:

> It's like Alcoholics Anonymous – it's like you go there with your shared problems ... and people give you these different ideas. ... you trial them and you take risks and you know most of the time these things work ... then you come back and you say 'yeah well that was good, it worked' ... and then new ideas come on ....

SIGs derived priorities for development variously from HMI or Ofsted visits, directly from the headteacher, through professional development planning, or from their own reflections and analysis. At their most effective, the SIGs were seen as major 'engines of change' in the schools, taking responsibility for staff training, co-ordinating weekly departmental meetings focused specifically on school improvement, developing behaviour policies, and perhaps most importantly bridging the divides between the academic and the pastoral, the rational and emotional. Students appreciated appropriate responses from staff, which to them were indicative of the school's worth:

> It is a good school because the teachers don't treat you badly. If you do something wrong they are pretty fair.

The SIGs' professional development work was well received in the schools, with some teachers describing it as 'inspirational' or the best form of INSET they had experienced. This was generally attributed to the sessions being run by teachers for teachers. As a teacher from The Ridings put it:

> There are far fewer staff out on courses. Most of the INSET is taken by SIG members and this is very good as the training is tailored to our needs. The quality of this INSET has been very high.

Year 11 students at another school remarked upon the improvement in teaching:

> *Teaching has got a lot better. It seems the teachers are more qualified to do the job because they know more. In Year 9 you had to copy, or do questions, out of a book. Now they explain things and they sound like they know what they are doing. They don't just stand with a book in their hand saying 'do that'. The teachers are more qualified because they have more money and can go on more courses.*

The SIGs also had an impact on their members and made a significant contribution to capacity building. The experience provided a collegial source of support which appears to have led to increased self-confidence, a sense of belonging and enhanced teacher professionalism. Teachers talked of feeling 'part of something bigger'. One young member of a SIG said after a SIG-led weekend conference, 'I now feel a part of the school'.

As a centrepiece of school improvement a body such as a SIG is a valuable, possibly even essential, lever for change. Such groups take different forms and go by different names in different countries. In Hong Kong, for example, they are known as the SIT, or School Improvement Team, sometimes they are top heavy with middle management, in other cases more like the Octet SIGs in drawing a representation from across the staff. A group of volunteers, able to work as a team, committed to improvement, with a clear remit and allocated time and support for their own professional development, can manifestly be a significant catalyst for improvement. While we do not need to look specifically to the SFECC project to reach this conclusion, it was one of the most tangible effects of the DfES intervention.

The idea of 'upskilling' middle managers and giving them a more significant role in the running of the school is a fairly conventional one; indeed the training of middle managers in the SFECC project was occurring at the same that the National College of School Leadership (NCSL) was introducing its 'Leading from the Middle' programme. Part of the rationale is that if middle managers can take on more of the day-to-day running of the school, the SLT may get more time and space for longer term strategic development. In addition, there is recognition that subject leaders have the expertise to drive developments in their subject area and to have a direct impact in the classroom.

The middle management programme used in the SFECC project was delivered through three two-day residential sessions. The focus of the training was on raising attainment, with module titles such as 'Constructing a raising attainment plan', 'Using data to inform the raising attainment plan' and 'Monitoring teacher performance and dealing with the outcome'. In addition to assisting subject leaders improve their own departments, they were also trained to be mentors to other subject leaders in the same school with a view to helping other departments improve.

There was a mixed response from the schools to the middle managers' training. The general feeling was that it was particularly suitable for inexperienced middle managers. One established head of department felt he hadn't learnt anything new, while another subject leader praised 'the quality of the delivery (and) the materials'. Crucially though, there was insufficient attention paid to how subject leader roles were going to be developed back in the schools. With no plan written into the training, neither from the DfES, nor organised by each school, the programme tended to be dead-end rather than dynamic. At several schools middle managers who had been trained and were keen to share their expertise were frustrated by a lack of backing from their senior leadership teams. The notion of mentoring also met with resistance. Some middle managers were simply sceptical about whether they could influence other departments; others felt uncomfortable about being presented as 'experts' and favoured a more collaborative approach. In several of the schools middle management developments stalled because of illness or staff turnover. Overall, the effects of the middle management programme were disappointing. Cross-departmental working is still so unusual in the secondary school that, unless opportunities are explicitly planned and built-in, development is unlikely to be sustained. One headteacher stated baldly that the middle management training was 'a wasted opportunity'.

Supporting heads and broadening leadership

The idea that for headteachers involvement in the SFECC initiative was a form of support and development surfaced in the early stages of the project. Simply being a part of the project helped them to gain knowledge, and was an impetus to entertain and take forward good ideas. Specific support took the form of three residential sessions spread over the duration of the project, together with other activities such as a dissemination day where heads met to share successful practice. There were also regular headteacher meetings, at least twice a term, organised by the DfES. Three of these were held at schools involved in the project, but most were held in London with a planned programme of input from the DfES. In general, heads welcomed the inputs at these sessions, but some felt that there was insufficient time for discussion and reflection. Certainly by the final year of the project they wanted to play a bigger part in setting the agenda for the meetings. A certain amount of networking also developed among the headteachers with informal contact and, in some instances, privately arranged meetings.

Broadening leadership teams through the appointment of extra members of staff was enabled in part by the additional funding from SFECC but also by headteachers' success in gaining funding from other sources. Five of the eight schools appointed an additional deputy or assistant headteacher, and a number of schools appointed data managers. In both The Ridings and St Albans one person combined the roles of deputy/assistant headteacher and data manager. Two of the schools also developed plans for an extended middle management group. Whilst the option of making additional appointments using SFECC funding was welcomed, headteachers recognised the short-term nature of the funding and were concerned about sustaining the posts beyond the project's end. Leadership in some schools developed simply as a result of having a full complement of staff for the first time in years, thus enabling a head to distribute leadership roles.

More dispersed leadership was possible through the development of the SIGs, to a limited extent through the development of the role of middle managers, and by virtue of a general increase in the proportion of adults other than teachers (AOTs). As in other schools, adults other than teachers were used increasingly in SFECC schools in a range of ways: as academic mentors, as individual learning coaches in welfare roles and as support for behaviour intervention. The Ridings, for example, moved from employing 3 to 28 mentors, and at Campion there was intensive use of Learning Support Assistants (financed in part through other sources of funding). While some roles were narrowly focused (for example learning mentors employed explicitly to improving GCSE examination performance), other AOT roles were wide-ranging, providing leadership in addressing the social and emotional needs of students and thus effectively increasing leadership density in the school.

Some difficulties

It is clearly evident that individual strands of the SFECC initiative were successful to differing degrees in the eight schools. The coherence and sustainability of the project as a whole is more open to question.

The project focused upon the classroom, yet it was teaching that was given centre stage, with much less emphasis on learning and learning theory, for which VAK and MI are weak substitutes. The assumption was that improving teaching through more structured and varied lessons provides a good starting point for improving learning; however, this is a contested proposition, at least without some detailed articulation as to how that conjunction might be achieved. The SIGs, together with the KS3 Strategy, successfully supported the adoption of surface practices such as icebreakers, plenaries, the three/four part lesson, objectives on the board, use of CATs data and a learning styles matrix. The enthusiasm with which the fast developing orthodoxy around learning styles was adopted was striking. However, the challenge was to deepen understanding and to support teachers in moving beyond formulaic approaches to more challenging evidence-led pedagogies. After two years there was little, if any, tangible evidence of a deeper impact on learning, although admittedly this is difficult to assess in the short term. The DfES's view of improvement as increased attainment at GCSE meant that inferences about deeper learning and the impact of professional development remained largely unaddressed.

The main thrust and energy of the project was directed towards professional development, with most of the centralised funding being used in staff training. Over the life of the project there were many examples of individuals benefiting from personal and career development. Given the turbulence of staffing in many of the SFECC schools, professional development could be seen as an incentive for staff to stay, and a reward for having done so, often through very difficult times. However, professional development that enhanced individuals' skills and confidence gave some of them increased 'market value'. One teacher said that while the project had been a 'fabulous CPD [Continuing Professional Development] opportunity' it had made these staff more visible and 'very attractive to other schools'. She added that everyone who was leaving at the end of the school year was moving on to promoted posts elsewhere. Since staff retention was already a major issue in several of these schools at the beginning of the project, and one which remained a concern in all of them, individual CPD was counter productive. Without professional development tied more strongly to organisational, rather than individual, enhancement, there is a danger of the new-found expertise being lost and the impact upon the school as a whole being significantly reduced. This was the case with the middle management training which failed to have significant impact, not necessarily because of the quality of the training, but because it was seen as an opportunity for some individuals, rather than a means to develop strategically the role of key groups of staff. Participants had a project to complete in their school, but this was perceived as their own and there was little linkage to the schools' wider improvement agendas. The mentoring aspect of the middle management training generally suffered from a lack of visible SLT commitment and the necessary circumstances in each school to provide the culture and time required for non-threatening cross-subject working.

Even where individuals stayed at the school and the focus of development was school-wide, as in the case of most of the SIGS, there was criticism that the SFECC training benefited only a limited number of staff and did not significantly build capacity across all the schools. There is always a delicate balance to be struck between creating an elite group and engendering a wider sense of ownership. A strong sense of bonding within an SIG is advantageous, particularly where the group is itself a learning community and is able to look outward as well as inward. Strong bonding also carries inherent dangers as discussed in Surowiecki's *The Wisdom of Crowds* (2004) in which he provides illustrations of how consensual groups build up resistance to alternative views and challenge. This is where social bridging comes into its own, as it can foster permeable borders within groups, creating spaces where other ideas are allowed to enter, and ideas can then flow out from the group to embrace others. It is a process through which capital is multiplied more widely within a school staff.

In contrast to the SIG training sessions which were attended predominantly by the same group of people, the middle management trainers spoke of the difficulties caused by different teachers attending parts of the same training programme. The choice of who should attend training appears to have been made at school rather than programme level, and some discontinuity in attendance was inevitable due, for example, to staff illness, resignation, and crises that arise quite frequently in schools on the edge. In addition, because the training events were frequently on Thursdays and Fridays, which are days sometimes associated with difficult behaviour in school, there was systematic absenteeism from the training – a source of some tension among schools, the providers and the DfES. It is no doubt frustrating for policy makers and programme managers when the strategic intent of their initiatives is not realised by the schools. The temptation is then to blame the schools for not adequately perceiving that intent, or failing to fulfil their side of the bargain, rather than questioning the model of training adopted.

The external training model was expensive, both in respect of external trainers and the social costs of withdrawing staff from the schools. All of the training sessions took place outside the school and in many cases staff had to travel long distances and spend significant time away from both their school and their home life. A concern shared by all of the schools was the effect on their functioning and on the students' learning. It was often the 'good teachers', who were absent in order to attend training, putting pressure on the staff remaining in school. It was also expensive in terms of employing supply teachers to cover, and disruptive to behaviour and learning. Students also expressed resentment when there was a lack of continuity amongst their teachers, especially nearing exam time.

It's not very fair on us, you know, when people like [Mrs X or Mr Y] go off and we get some Australian woman who doesn't know anything about the exams and doesn't know how to give us the help we need.

Teachers also commented on this:

It's an issue that the week before GCSE exams started, four members of staff are out. You have got to question the timing of that ... you know I missed two GCSE geography classes.

SIGs were deemed successful in spite of the fact that schools struggled to send SIG members to every training session, and considering that two schools were regularly absent. This seems to suggest that it is possible to foster a SIG spirit within a school without extensive outside support, raising questions about the scale and type of training necessary for success. What is clear is that if the SIG model is to be successful in the long term, capacity has to move beyond the enthusiasms of specific individuals, and the SIG's values and practices – how it works and what it stands for – need to be embedded in the culture of the school. The group itself needs to develop an 'organisational memory' and thus a momentum and vitality beyond its individual members, an issue sharpened as experienced members leave and new members join. For a school to foster and sustain a group such as a SIG requires a cycle of development, quality planning time, risk-taking, monitoring, maintenance and feedback loops, all needing time and support from leadership.

The policy context in which the SFECC schools were working meant that they had to adjust to directives coming from various directions: from the DfES, from local authority advisers, HMI and Ofsted inspectors. Running parallel, and sometimes weaving in with the developments offered within the SFECC project, have been a plethora of other staff development initiatives, for example the Graduate Teacher Programme and training offered through the local authorities' employment of Advanced Skills Teachers. At the same time, schools were bidding for funding from a variety of sources simply to remain viable. One of the significant external initiatives to impact upon the schools was the KS3 Strategy with its accompanying close monitoring. While much of the SFECC training was complementary to the strategy, a remark by one headteacher is revealing: in 2004–2005 the SIG was going to focus on more practical matters 'and not on university stuff'.

A measure of a school's capacity-building and future sustainability is the extent to which it is able to integrate all these various strands and embed new initiatives into its planning and improvement strategies. While the SFECC project did not attempt to help schools individually weave these various initiatives together into a purposeful and coherent strategy, it did aim to provide the enhancement of expertise that would enable schools to meet these challenges more robustly.

Cold feet and hard lessons

The initial thinking behind the SFECC project had been bold. What was implemented was a more watered down version of the original plans. Originally SFECC was planned to last for five years, a time-span which would have allowed developments in learning and teaching to have maximum effect on students who were in Year 7 at the beginning of the project, and which would have provided a longitudinal view of the cumulative change in the school. It also would have been a realistic time-span for bringing about transformation. However, in the event the project only lasted three years, and was only fully active for two of those. There was considerable slippage in putting policy into practice and some of the radicalism of the early days had disappeared. Looking back, the tensions were clearly there at the project's inception.

The radicalism shifted markedly during the early stages of the project and quickly settled into a more conventional package of support. Even by the time the project had begun ambition had been scaled back to a more explicit focus on attainment and the schools 'turning themselves around', as this extract from the White Paper *Schools Achieving Success* (DfES, 2001b) makes clear:

6.14 *From September 2001 we are funding a pilot project with eight well managed secondary schools ... We want the schools to find new ways to use the skills of their teachers and other adults so that they have the capacity to turn themselves around and raise the attainment of their pupils. For example, the project will support teachers to plan together and observe each other's teaching, so that they learn and develop together; it will test the effect of radically reduced class sizes.* (DfES, 2001: 50–1)

In the event, the promise of 'radically reduced class sizes' was not delivered, and was only to be found in the RML programme introduced as part of the project.

It is not simply that the DfES got cold feet, though as one senior member of the DfES explained, the Civil Service is naturally 'risk averse' in spending public money. The schools themselves, most of whom already had strong links with their local communities, were cautious about some of the proposals, such as shifting to a fundamental restructuring of the school year. So the changes which actually occurred in the schools during the project were more extensions of existing activities, such as breakfast clubs, after school and weekend activities, and summer holiday literacy classes for incoming Year 7 students. Plans to exchange staff between the schools were shelved at an early stage.

There was also a perception at the DfES that at the beginning of the project the eight schools lacked strategic capacity, and were dependent on the DfES team to provide direction, as evidenced by a senior civil servant at the DfES:

I'm not sure but we certainly didn't see our involvement as being as great as it turned out. We thought that there would be more proactivity from the schools themselves. We thought they might appoint people with the additional funding. Appoint an extra deputy or whatever to run the project within the school and liaise with the other schools, but they haven't really done that to the extent ... they haven't taken leadership and ownership of the project in the way that we thought that they might do.

There were also concerns at the DfES at the beginning of the project that the schools would spend money on add-ons and fail to adopt the radical change being asked of them, not least because of the everyday challenges in all these schools, and the additional pressures some were facing. The Ridings School, for example, had just come out of Special Measures in January 2001 and Phoenix School was still designated as having 'serious weaknesses' in February 2001.

Can governments change schools?

Can governments change schools through externally-led initiatives such as the SFECC project? This intervention was premised on the notion that if everything we have learned about school improvement could be applied with funding, support and training, these schools on the edge would show dramatic gains and wider policy lessons would be adduced. Although it came out after the project had finished, the publication *School Improvement – Lessons from Research* (Hopkins et al., 2005) captures these school improvement assumptions well. Hopkins summarises four key points, all of which are applicable when considering the SFECC project.

Firstly, it is 'at the level of the individual classroom teacher that most of the differences between schools seem to occur' (Hopkins et al., 2005: 4). The implication is that the emphasis of school improvement should be upon teachers and their work in the classroom. This premise is derived from effectiveness and improvement studies which show, perhaps not surprisingly, that the teacher effect is larger than the school effect and that much effort can be wasted on things which have little to do with teaching and learning. Whether this is as true for schools on the edge as it might be elsewhere is a question we raised in the previous chapter. Even if it is accepted that teachers should be the prime focus for school improvement efforts, questions remain about how best to achieve the outcome. How can government-led intervention strategies reach *every* teacher in a school? And to what degree can all teachers be transformed not only in teaching skill but also in terms of their disposition to be sufficiently risk-taking to confront inappropriate curriculum and testing? Would this imply direct and intensive 'training' of every teacher, bearing in mind the continual turnover of staff? Or the cascading of training through key staff such as mentors and consultants? Or the creation of enough space, resource and support for collaborative lesson planning, peer observation, rigorous and sustained self-evaluation? Even posing the questions exposes some of the complexities. The SFECC intervention did focus much of its energy on classroom practice, but this was primarily through the training of senior and middle leaders and school improvement group members. None of these, in themselves or in concert, could be guaranteed to bring about the depth of penetration on students' learning needed to revitalise and energise disaffected and alienated young people.

The second premise put forward by Hopkins et al. was that 'what pupils learn in school is partly dependent on what they bring to school in terms of their family and individual social and economic circumstances. Deprivation is still by far the biggest determinant of educational success' (2005: 6). Juxtaposing 'partly dependent' and 'biggest determinant' is a position which sits uncomfortably on the fence. At one end of the spectrum there are children whose families can give them such strong support from the earliest age that they arrive at the school gates able to read fluently, with a wealth of knowledge of the world, eager to learn and impervious to the frustrations that classroom learning often entails. At the other end are children whose families do not have the resources to provide that early years support. In cases where poverty brings with it the despair of drug or alcohol addiction, children can be so psychologically damaged as to make 'access' to the curriculum an irrelevance. Some commentators have concluded that there are strong arguments for investing effort in the wider community and on the kind of inter-agency support now advocated by *Every Child Matters* and *Youth Matters* policy initiatives. Yet the SFECC project was entirely focused upon the schools. There was little additional community activity as a direct result of the project.

The third premise was that 'sustained improvement over a period of years is unusual, and of course, year to year some schools will fall back' (Hopkins et al., 2005: 6). This places a premium on school improvement efforts to produce sustainability. Yet great store was placed on each school's annual test results, which are themselves only a very limited measure of a school's achievements (an issue focused on in greater depth in Chapter 6). Struggling schools in general, and schools involved in SFECC in particular, were subject to frequent monitoring by HMI, and the pressure for short term tangible evidence of 'improvement' was immense. Students were acutely aware of this, commenting:

Teachers are putting a lot of pressure on you to get the grades, and it is shattering for you and the teachers. Since Year 8 the fun of learning has gone out of things really. We've hardly gone on any trips, and it's 'you must do this, you must do that …'. There is so much pressure. It is not fair on us or the teachers because they are really really exhausted and it's hard work for everyone. It was laid back for the first couple of years – now it is stricter for the present Year 7s and Year 8s. They're trying harder to start them early so they get a better grade. There has been very little fun for the last couple of years. It is no fun but we keep trying and working because of the thought of achieving something, and we want our GCSEs.

Finally, 'Schools that generate sustained improvement tend to act strategically' (Hopkins et al., 2005: 7). The dilemma for the Octet schools, was that what Gray et al. (1999) refer to as short-term tactical measures, were seen an imperative for survival. It is precisely those schools on the very edge of acceptable performance that are expected to prove themselves in the conventional currency of GCSE and point scores. As headteachers frequently testified, they had very short-term targets and some senior leaders saw this as a moral conflict that they wrestled with on a daily basis. Should they deploy the best teachers and invest the greatest efforts on those young people most likely to pay dividends in terms of critical benchmark?

Can governments change schools? National Curriculum, Key Stage testing and Key Stage Strategies demonstrate something of the deep impact on school practice. However, there is little evidence to support the belief that a set of improvement measures can be applied to schools living life continually on the edge. Prescription and straitjacket policies can not only prove demoralising for young people, cast as failures, but equally demoralising for 'failing' schools and for teachers whose enthusiasm for teaching has slowly been extinguished (MacBeath et al., 2006). Had some of the radical restructuring proposals envisioned in the original 'grand' plan been realised, things might have been very different. The attack of 'cold feet' by timorous and risk-averse civil servants tells its own powerful story.

The problem is that no matter how great the improvement in teaching or how enhanced the skills of senior leaders, middle leaders, teachers and SIGs, these schools are located in the force field of external pressures greater than the impetus and capacity for internal school improvement. The ambiguous improvement data, presented in the next chapter, does not deny or undermine all the good things that Octet schools have achieved, the pride students, teachers and parents have in their schools, and the remarkable success of some young people whose success against the odds is celebrated in the photographs, testimonies and student work which adorn corridors, offices and classrooms. Many of these schools are 'good' or even 'outstanding' in ways unrecognised and uncelebrated by performance tables. Their quality lies in the commitment, imagination and determination they show in persisting against the odds and giving hope to many young people who entered their doors with little hope or expectation. Some of these schools and classrooms are truly inspirational places to visit. They deserve better.

QUESTIONS FOR REFLECTION AND DISCUSSION

1. Using ICT in new ways was central to this project. Is the use of new forms of ICT going to change education in fundamental ways?
2. Caution and risk-taking are key ideas associated with the project. To what extent can schools on the edge be expected to take risks? To what extent are they themselves risk averse? How could they have been better supported?
3. The development of more democratic forms of leadership, with new-found expertise crossing traditional hierarchical boundaries, was the unequivocal success of the project. How is such leadership maintained and developed in the long term, when particular project funding ceases?
4. Given the same level of funding (£6 million for eight schools over three years), how would you have spent the money?

Note

1 A Teachers' TV video with a four way debate among reading experts can be downloaded from http://www.teachers.tv/strandProgrammeVideo.do?strandId=59957&transmission ProgrammeId=275316

6

Measuring Improvement

This chapter examines GCSE performance in the Octet schools over the length of the project comparing:

- each school's own performance with their own previous best;
- pupil progress in terms of 'added value';
- the Octet schools with 'similar' schools;
- the SFECC Project with other policy initiatives.

For many people the question of whether an innovation has worked boils down to a single question: did the schools' measured performance improve? This is a deceptively simple question to pose; it is rather more difficult to answer. But, for those who like to keep things simple, a positive answer can be provided. The schools' results went up. Furthermore, some part of that improvement can almost certainly be attributed to their involvement in the SFECC initiative.

Interpreting statistics, unfortunately, is rarely that straightforward. The schools' results do not 'speak for themselves'; they demand interpretation. Different approaches tend to yield different results and so it proved with these schools. Furthermore, many of the techniques readily available for evaluating schools' performance do not easily lend themselves to the rather different circumstances of schools on the edge. As one of us has argued elsewhere, the problems of evaluating schools serving disadvantaged communities have been under-estimated (Gray, 2005). This chapter focuses on the eight schools but it relates, of course, to the wider question of the strengths and limitations of the information currently available publicly to draw inferences about schools' performance.

The nature and limitations of traditional yardsticks

Most commentators would agree on one thing. When the SFECC schools joined the project their academic performance was 'low' and there was probably 'room for improvement' in all of them. Indeed, they were selected for participation for precisely this reason. 'Low' performance, on this occasion, was defined as having 15% or fewer of their pupils achieve 5 or more A*–C grades (5+ A*–C) in the GCSE examinations they took at the age of 16–plus in the years 1999 and 2000, the so-called 'headline' statistic for this age group. The schools varied in the extent to which they fell short of this hurdle. A couple were hovering just below it; in other cases, however, where the percentages were in single figures, even reaching 15% may have seemed quite a stiff target. In fact, the government made it clear at the time that it would shortly be raising its expectations still further – 20% was to be seen as the minimum.

Broadly speaking, schools performing below the 15% level fell, at that time, into the bottom 5% of schools in terms of the national distribution of performance. The percentages 15% and 20% have a commonsense appeal about them. However, they do not map neatly onto any underlying distribution of schools. In both cases, judged against national averages at least, they could be said to justify the label of 'low performance'. But how formidable a target they actually represented, differed across the schools. All schools in the project were being exhorted to raise their performance by at least 50% but, in some cases, the expectations generated from these headline statistics were substantially greater; schools where the percentages of pupils getting over this particular hurdle were in single figures were being enjoined to *more than double* their performance over a relatively short period of time.

The role of 'public opinion' in target-setting should not be under-estimated. The 5+ A*–C hurdle is the one to which most attention is given by the media when reporting the annual performance tables. Nonetheless, it remains a relatively 'high' one; nationally, for every young person who reaches it there is another who doesn't. Arguably, for schools in 'exceptionally challenging' circumstances, a 'lower' hurdle, such as the proportions *not* securing any passes (at any level) at GCSE might have been relevant. In 1998, three years before the project began there had been significant minorities of pupils (up to one in five) at each of the schools who had secured no exam qualifications whatsoever. This contrasts with the position nationally where around 7% were in this position. There are signs that the schools were already taking this issue seriously; indeed in 2000, the year before the project started, most of them had reduced their figures to below 10%. Nonetheless, there was considerable variation between schools; whilst a couple ensured that almost everyone secured something, two schools continued to have significant proportions of pupils (26% and 19%) with no passes whatsoever.

One of the problems of relying on these traditional measures of school performance is that, in the process of summarising performance, a large amount of information can be lost. Most obviously, the 5+ A*–C measure ignores pupil performances which fall short – by whatever distance. A pupil securing four grade Cs and a D, for example, is not included; neither is one who secures nothing. Concern about the crudeness of such measures has led to the inclusion of the so-called GCSE Points Score in the performance tables. This measure provides a score for every grade awarded to a pupil at GCSE. The national average for all pupils in 2001 totalled just over 39 points. The schools in the project, by contrast, hovered around a figure of just over 21 points in the same year, ranging from a low of 19.4 to a high of 24.1. Compared with the national average all the schools were lagging a long way behind (by some 18 points); just as significantly, perhaps, within the group there were also differences.

There are different ways of expressing gaps of this size but, in substantive terms, whereas pupils nationally were securing the equivalent of seven or eight grade C passes, those in the project schools were getting the equivalent of about four and these are much more likely to have included some D and E grades in their profiles. Comparing just the schools in the project, the range between them was equivalent to the pupils in the highest-attaining school securing one grade better in five subjects than pupils attending the school at the other extreme.

Four frameworks for measuring 'success'

Acknowledging, for a moment, that it could be argued that all the project schools were 'low-attaining' in relation to the national average and, potentially, 'underperforming', what might it be reasonable to expect from them by way of performance and, consequently, improvement over the three or four years of the project?

There are several ways of answering this question. The first is to compare each school with its *own previous best performance* in recent years. Has it managed to improve on this and, equally importantly, are there any tentative signs that this improvement has continued? Is the school, in other words, on an upward trajectory? This approach essentially compares the school's performance with itself.

Second, how much *progress* are the pupils making from where they started? What evidence is there that the school is 'adding value'? This is a comparative judgement in which the reference points are based on looking at the progress of comparable pupils in comparable schools.

Both these judgements can be made, albeit rather crudely, from the published statistics available in the annual performance tables. However, two other questions also merit attention. Both rely on the idea that the project constituted a kind of 'quasi-experiment' in which the group of schools recruited to the project are compared with other schools which might, in other circumstances, have been recruited. This third approach involves the notion of a *comparison group* and is based on identifying schools which are initially 'similar' to the schools in the project in terms of overall levels of performance and the nature of their intakes. Their subsequent performance, as a group, is then compared with that of the project schools. Did they make the same or greater progress than the comparison group? There are practical limitations in the extent to which notions of 'similarity' can be realised on the available data but we believe a good approximation is possible.

Our fourth strategy *compares* the success of various *policy initiatives* directed at raising schools' performance. The eight schools might have become involved in one of several other initiatives including, possibly, the Special Measures programme, the Fresh Start programme or, more recently, that related to Academies. How did their progress within the SFECC project compare with that of other schools who entered these other programmes?

We would argue that each of these four approaches has something to contribute to answering our over-arching question about how well the schools did. Of course, each of them has some limitations. By combining them, however, the possibility of a more firmly-grounded judgement emerges.

Improving on past performance

A variety of measures is potentially available for capturing schools' exam performance. For purposes of clarity we confine ourselves here to just three measures: the percentages of pupils obtaining 5+ A*–C grades, the percentage obtaining no passes, and each school's average Exam Points Score.

5+ A*–C passes

When the schools were selected, none of them met the government's declared target of securing at least 15% of their pupils achieving the 5+ A*–C grades. Consequently, securing this 'threshold' became a driving concern. When the project commenced, one or two of the schools were already within striking distance of it whilst two or three had a long way to go.

Before addressing the question of whether the schools reached the new threshold, therefore, it is important to establish whether they were able to improve substantially on their own recent best performance. Figure 6.1 covers the period 1998 to 2005. The evidence in this graph suggests that all eight of the schools had improved on their previous best performances achieved in the three years prior to the project. In six out of the eight cases this was by a substantial margin. In terms of the government's threshold target of 20% of pupils reaching this particular hurdle by 2001, just one school had attained it; in 2002 two. By 2003 the total reaching this level was six. This is important because, as the DfES clearly indicated in its

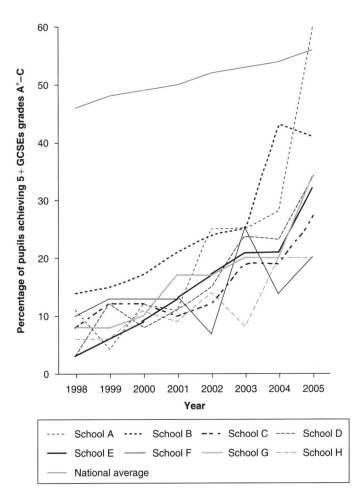

Figure 6.1 Percentages of pupils obtaining 5+ A*–C grades (or equivalent) 1998–2005

commentary on the 2004 Annual Performance Tables, 'results for 2004 [would] not necessarily be fully comparable with results for earlier years because of the inclusion of a wider range of qualifications' in the indicator.

The overall position did not change very much in 2004. Six schools reached the target although these were a slightly different six from the previous year. The two schools which did not reach this level were amongst the schools which had the furthest to go from their respective starting points. The results for 2005 showed a similar number of schools reaching the target but some were now exceeding it by a considerable margin.

The decision to widen the range of qualifications taken into account for this indicator was taken independently of this evaluation. It will doubtless have improved the position of the SFECC and similar schools involved in presenting

Table 6.1   Percentage of pupils by school securing no passes at any level at GCSE (or equivalent) 1998–2005

	A(%)	B(%)	C(%)	D(%)	E(%)	F(%)	G(%)	H(%)
1998	14	14	16	26	18	7	12	11
1999	11	22	3	13	22	2	11	10
2000	0	4	26	19	9	1	10	13
2001	4	10	13	11	23	4	9	17
2002	0	24	10	14	7	9	2	14
2003	2	13	26	18	1	3	2	16
2004*	0	10	1	12	7	7	3	5
2005**	1	7	5	13	4	3	5	8

* The figures for 2004 take account of a broader range of qualifications, whereas those for earlier years relate to pupils securing no passes at GCSE alone.
** From 2005 percentages are for pupils at the end of Key Stage 4, *not* pupils aged 15 as previously.

Source: DfES

their pupils for a wider range of qualifications than GCSE alone. Unfortunately we are not in a position to disentangle its effects from the data currently available. Whatever the case, its impact on the schools' trajectories appears overall to have been relatively modest; in only two cases does there appear to have been a significant boost to recorded achievement levels between 2003 and 2004 (see Figure 6.1). By 2005, however, the impact was more marked: six schools had taken an apparently sizeable step forward.

No passes

The proportions obtaining no passes (at any grade) at GCSE or (for 2004) any equivalent qualification provides a lower threshold whose significance will vary from school to school. Three of the schools had significant minorities of pupils not reaching this level of performance (see Table 6.1). Again, the extent to which the figures fluctuated during this pre-project period from one year to the next should be noted.

By 2003 pupils in four of the schools were almost all securing some form of qualification. The figures for 2004 suggest a certain determination on the Octet's part with respect to this measure as the majority of schools pushed forward, probably indicating that their efforts had not previously been captured by the statistics which were confined to GCSE alone. The results for 2005 resemble those for 2004.

Interpreting figures relating to the 'no passes' indicator can be problematic. There is growing recognition that there may be valid educational reasons for excluding some pupils from calculation of the statistics. Schools may already exclude 'refugees', for example, and new arrivals with limited skills in English language. The addition of vocational qualifications as 'recognised qualifications' to those to be counted also complicates the position. 'Improvements' in this area may be partly a matter of accounting practice – qualifications which were not previously included subsequently were included without there necessarily being any change in practice. Furthermore, schools facing exceptionally challenging circumstances will almost certainly have some pupils for whom *any* type of formal qualification represents a comparatively high target. Schools' decisions about the extent to which such pupils on the margins are to be entered for formal qualifications can have a significant impact on the overall picture.

Exam Points Scores

The GCSE/GNVQ Points Score is a measure which attempts to give credit to all levels of performance for which a grade has been given and not just the higher grades. However, this indicator has been subject to changing definitions over time. In 2001 the Points Score measure was 'uncapped', that is, all a pupil's results were allowed to contribute to the total (see Table 6.2). In 2002 and 2003 the results were 'capped', being confined to a pupil's best eight results. The DfES has stated that the 'main reason for publishing a capped point score was to ensure consistency with the output scores used in value-added analyses'. Whatever the reasons, the outcome makes our task of drawing conclusions more complicated.

How far 'capping' will have affected the results of the vast majority of pupils in the SFECC schools is unclear but, from our explorations, it seems likely that only small minorities will have had more than eight results from which to choose. Whatever the case, for 2004 a decision was made 'after consultation by the Secretary of State … to publish an uncapped standalone Point Score' whilst continuing to use a 'capped Points Score' for value-added calculations. Furthermore, a new scoring system was introduced as part of these changes. To facilitate comparisons over time, we have attempted to recalculate what the results would have been, using the previous system although our calculations involve, of necessity, some approximations (Table 6.2).

Table 6.2   GCSE/GNVQ (or equivalent) Points Scores by school 2001–2005

	A	B	C	D	E	F	G	H
2001	21.1	24.1	21.8	19.8	19.4	21.0	23.6	21.0
2002*	26.2	20.7	22.2	19.2	14.2	20.8	23.1	20.9
2003*	25.7	25.7	21.0	18.7	20.9	22.8	24.3	18.2
2004**	286	303	213	192	168	227	243	209
2004***	32.4	34.0	24.8	20.4	16.6	23.5	25.7	22.1
2005**	367	309	215	221	192	257	267	217
2005***	43.1	35.0	22.9	24.0	20.1	27.7	29.4	24.4

  * = capped scores; 2001, 2004 and 2005 were uncapped.
 ** These figures relate to a wider range of qualifications (not just GCSEs) and are based around a newly-introduced scoring system.
*** We have recalculated these figures in an attempt to use the same metric for the 2004 and 2005 figures as those employed in previous years – they are, of necessity, approximations.

Source: DfES

The changes in the ways in which the different measures were constructed across the years makes strict comparisons difficult. Comparing the positions in 2001 and 2005, it seems safe to say that in six cases the signs were positive: in three cases the increases were substantial whilst in the other three they were more modest. In two cases, however, there is little evidence of movement.

Trends over time

The capacity not only to secure improvements but to sustain them provides a stiff test of the schools' performance. In Table 6.3 we have calculated the 'rates of change' year on year occurring amongst the schools in relation to the 5+ A*–C indicator. By way of explanation, if a school improved its results from 10% to 12% over the course of a year, this would be recorded as a 20% increase. Schools which manage to secure positive steps over time are likely to have found ways of developing the ideal of 'continuous improvement'.

Careful inspection of the figures in Table 6.3 suggests that steady improvement over time was mostly missing amongst the schools in the three years prior to the project (i.e. up to and including 2001); in most cases their results fluctuated from one year to the next whilst remaining generally 'low' by comparison with national averages. The overall picture remained much the same by 2005. There was evidence of some kind of trend in four schools (the year-on-year percentages were generally positive or only marginally negative in one particular year).

Table 6.3   Year-on-year percentage changes in proportions of pupils obtaining 5+ A*–C – (or equivalent) 1998–2005

	A(%)	B(%)	C(%)	D(%)	E(%)	F(%)	G(%)	H(%)
1998								
1999	−64	7	50	300	100	30	0	0
2000	200	13	0	−33	50	0	25	83
2001	−8	24	−17	38	44	0	70	−18
2002	127	14	20	36	−46	31	0	56
2003	0	4	58	60	257	24	18	−43
2004*	12	72	0	−4	−44	0	0	150
2005**	114	−5	42	48	43	52	70	0

From 2004 a wider range of qualifications have been included by the DfES in the 5+ A–C grades indicator.
**From 2005 percentages are for pupils at the end of KS4 *not* pupils aged 15 as previously.

Source: DfES

One other note of caution is necessary at this point. The 5+ A*–C measure has been criticised recently for not being sufficiently discriminating in relation to the inclusion of 'core' subjects. This has led to demands that passes in English and maths should be specifically included in the measure. Responding to pressure, the DfES recently recalculated the figures for the last four years going back to the year 2001/02. The introduction of this measure has had some impact at national level. Whereas, in 2005, some 57% of pupils secured this level of performance when grades in all subjects are counted, this fell to 45% when maths and English were included.

The effects in the SFECC schools were more dramatic. Whereas, again in 2005, just under 34% reached the hurdle when all subjects were included, this figure fell to just under 14% when maths and English were included. The results for individual schools are presented in Table 6.4 which juxtaposes the outcomes using the two measures.

It can be seen that in some cases the picture that emerges is rather different. Only two of the schools managed to sustain a continuous upward trend in the proportions of pupils securing grades C or better when maths and English are included; in the remaining six there was no discernible upward trend. In four of the schools the proportions were broadly the same in 2005 as in 2002, or had declined, whilst in three they had increased substantially.

Table 6.4 Percentages of pupils including maths and English amongst their 5+ A*–C grades (or equivalent) 2002–2005

	A	B	C	D	E	F	G	H
2002	**20**	**14**	**12**	**4**	**1**	**14**	**13**	**5**
	25	24	12	15	7	17	17	14
2003	**16**	**15**	**16**	**8**	**10**	**16**	**15**	**6**
	25	25	19	25	25	21	20	8
2004*	**23**	**20**	**18**	**11**	**5**	**10**	**20**	**19**
	28	43	19	23	14	21	20	20
2005**	**17**	**15**	**6**	**13**	**5**	**13**	**22**	**13**
	60	41	27	34	20	32	34	20

Figures in bold indicate percentages securing grades A*–C in maths and English amongst their five; figures not in bold indicate overall percentages obtaining 5+ A*–C grades at GCSE.

 * From 2004 a wider range of qualifications have been included by the DfES in the 5+ A*–C grades indicator.

** From 2005 percentages are for pupils at the end of KS4 *not* pupils aged 15 as previously.

Source: DfES

Perhaps the most obvious message to emerge from Table 6.4, however, is the extent to which judgements about the schools' progress are heavily dependent on the weight that is given to the maths/English criterion. In one case the differences seem very substantial indeed. On closer inspection, however, the introduction of this measure does not appear to have had much impact on the rank ordering of the eight schools – although it does focus attention on a different school at the top end as the one being potentially of most interest.

Value-added approaches to assessing performance

There has been considerable interest in the last few years in adopting value-added approaches to assessing schools' performances. These attempt to estimate how far pupils in a particular school have progressed from their initial starting points. Since 2002 these estimates have been included in the Performance Tables. These have been based on the assumption that the figures will be centred around 100 although in practice the median score fell just below 100 (in 2004 the system was rescaled to centre scores around 1000). Thus, a score well above 100 indicates that the pupils in a particular school have been making considerably more progress than would have been predicted from knowledge of their starting points, whilst a score well below 100 indicates that they have made considerably less progress. A high score on this scale (placing a school in the highest 5% of schools nationally) would be somewhere over 105 whilst a low score (placing a school in the lowest 5% nationally) would be 95 or below.

Table 6.5 shows the results for the project schools over the period 2002–2005. Given that the baseline year for the project was 2001 and that the value-added figures record progress from Key Stage 3 to GCSE (or equivalent), the figures for 2002 will only partially have been influenced by the project's activities.

Value-added perspectives do not, of course, necessarily provide the same picture of a school's performance as figures which do not take account of pupils' progress and it should be noted that, before the project started, two of the schools appeared to be performing above national expectations on VA whilst a third was meeting them. The figures for 2005 provide a slightly more optimistic picture than 2002: three of the schools exceeded national expectations, three fell below them whilst the remaining two were around the national average. In total four schools appear to have improved their value-added positions over the course of the project whilst none declined.

The figures in Table 6.5 relate to pupil progress from Key Stage 3 to GCSE. This is a relatively short period of schooling, albeit an extremely important one. Table 6.6 shows the position for those young people who were in the schools from Key Stage 2 to GCSE, a period of five years in total. These young people will have been exposed to initiatives emerging from the project during the latter half of their school careers. The figures give a more pessimistic picture of the progress being made. Only one of the schools seems to have been performing at levels commensurate with national expectations, whilst the performance of five of the remaining seven placed them in the bottom quarter of performance; three of these schools were to be found amongst the lowest 5% of schools nationally on this measure.

Overall, the picture generated by the value-added measures is a patchy one. At the beginning of the project, pupils in the majority of the schools were making

Table 6.5 Value-added scores between Key Stage 3 and GCSE 2002–2005

	A	B	C	D	E	F	G	H
2002	101.3	99.3	102.4	94.1	93.8	93.2	97.9	94.6
2003	101.8	104.5	100.9	92.0	96.7	94.1	99.8	94.5
2004*	1024	1012	987	936	949	971	975	986
2004**	102.4	101.2	98.7	93.6	94.9	97.1	97.5	98.6
2005**	1044	1020	1027	961	948	990	980	973
2005***	104.4	102.0	102.7	96.1	94.8	99.0	98.0	97.3

  *From 2004 a wider range of qualifications have been included by the DfES in constructing this indicator; however, it should be noted that the 2004 measure remains capped.

 **From 2005 the figures are for pupils at the end of Key Stage 4, *not* pupils aged 15 as previously.

***These figures rescale the published figures for 2004 and 2005; they are based on assumptions about the need for a high degree of continuity between the scoring systems adopted in 2003 and 2004.

Source: DfES

Table 6.6 Value-added scores between Key Stage 2 and GCSE in 2004 and 2005

	A	B	C	D	E	F	G	H
2004*	998	966	950	906	918	931	965	951
2005	1002	962	989	920	916	936	973	948

*From 2004 a wider range of qualifications have been included by the DfES in constructing this indicator.

Source: DfES

less progress than might have been expected. Three years later the same observation held true. Only two of the eight were performing as expected or better, two were still lagging well behind whilst the remaining four were performing below expectations. In just two cases was there any obvious upward movement suggesting an improvement in their value-added positions.

Drawing conclusions about overall improvement

Using a number of indicators to compare the schools' performance is appropriate but makes the task of reaching an overall judgement about the extent of improvement difficult. We experimented with a number of different ways of grouping the measures but eventually concluded that the measures of trends over time and value-added should probably be given greater prominence. Eventually we concluded that the schools could be divided into three broad groups:

A) where there was evidence of a positive change in performance on (most of) the indicators which suggested that the changes had been substantial and also provided some signs of upward trends over time and of improvements in value-added;

B) where there was evidence of a positive change in performance on (some of) the indicators but where the scale of improvement was less substantial and there was less evidence of upward trends or improvements in value-added; and

C) where the evidence, whilst generally indicative of some improvement, did not amount to convincing evidence of changes in performance over time or of increases in value-added.

Grouping the schools in this way did not prove straightforward. Eventually we concluded that two schools fell into Group A where there was evidence of substantial improvement in GCSE period over the period 2001–05 including signs of upward trends on the key indictors; two fell into Group B where the scale of the improvement was generally in an upward direction; and the remaining four fell into Group C where the evidence for change was generally rather modest.

Looking at the schools in isolation from the system of which they are a part provides only a partial picture for the purposes of policy development. In the next sections we start to address the question of what might have happened to the schools if they had not been involved in the SFECC initiative and, more generally, how the outcomes of the project seem to compare with other policy developments that have been launched in recent years.

Comparing changes in performance with 'similar' schools

In reviewing the performance of the SFECC schools we felt it would be useful to have some 'comparison' schools against which to judge progress. These would be schools facing similar challenges in similar circumstances. They would not, of course, have been involved in the SFECC initiative although they might have taken part in other projects with similar or related concerns. The comparison group schools are not a 'control group' in the strict sense that this term is usually used. The SFECC schools were deliberately selected to participate in the project and consequently no random assignment of other schools to a control group was deemed appropriate.

In identifying a comparison group we tried to match each of the project schools with a number of others. Clearly key considerations were that the matched schools were comparable in terms of previous academic attainment, experiencing similar levels of social disadvantage and working with similar proportions of pupils judged to have Special Educational Needs (SEN).

There was a further consideration which we judged to be at least as important as the three criteria mentioned above and probably more important – namely the schools' respective 'value-added' contributions or 'effectiveness' at the time the project started. For this purpose we used data for 2001 available from the Pupil Level Annual Schools Census (PLASC) on pupils' progress from Key Stage 3 to GCSE. For each of the SFECC schools we attempted to find at least three 'matched' schools based on the application of the following criteria in order of priority:

(a) levels of pupil progress judged in terms of 'value-added' residuals;
(b) evidence of 'low' overall performance in terms of headline statistics;
(c) levels of social disadvantage in terms of the proportions on free school meals; and
(d) the proportions of pupils judged by their schools to have Special Educational Needs.

In addition, we tried to include at least one school for each of the eight which took some account of its organisational type (for example boys-only, secondary modern and sports specialist). When we applied these three criteria in combination, they reduced the list of schools potentially recruitable to the comparison group rather dramatically; in practice, our comparison group contained virtually all the other schools in England in similar positions.

We achieved a good match in most respects. The figures for the SFECC schools and the comparison group were almost identical for three of the four criteria outlined above in relation to their positions. It proved more difficult, however, to secure close matches on the fourth, the percentages of pupils judged to have SEN. The application of the first three criteria reduced the potential sample of schools close to the minimum figures we felt desirable and strict application of the fourth resulted in the group of comparison schools being reduced still further and well below the numbers we considered viable. Consequently the proportions of young people judged to have SEN was higher in the SFECC schools than in the comparison group (an average of 51% compared with 37%). We do not judge this difference to be particularly significant as individual schools can decide for themselves what proportion of their pupils are identified by this measure. Clearly across both groups of schools their perceptions were that sizeable proportions of their pupils fell into this category.

The comparison group originally contained 24 schools but by 2004 one school had been renamed/closed so no data were available. Consequently the comparison group finally contained 23 schools. Table 6.7 shows the results for the SFECC and comparison group in relation to the 5+ A*–C measure. Over this period the national percentages reaching this hurdle rose from 50% to just under 54%, a rise of some four percentage points.

Table 6.7   Proportions of pupils achieving 5+ A*–C grades (or equivalent) in the SFECC and Comparison Schools 2001–2005

	National(%)	SFECC(%)	Comparison Schools(%)
2001	50.0	13.2	15.5
2002	52.0	17.2	18.8
2003	52.9	20.7	24.3
2004*	53.7	23.5	26.8
2005**	57.1	33.7	33.5

From 2004 a wider range of qualifications have been included by the DfES in the 5+ A–C grades (or equivalent) indicator.

**The 2005 percentages are for pupils at the end of Key Stage 4, *not* aged 15 as previously. The figures in this table have been weighted to take account of differences in cohort size across the schools.

Source: DfES

The average for the SFECC schools rose by some three or four percentage points a year. Over the period 2001 to 2004, covering the baseline year and the three years when project activity was most intense, the increase amounted to some ten percentage points. The average for the comparison schools also rose by a similar amount. For both groups of schools the rates of increase were very similar. Both groups secured further improvements during 2005 and ahead of national trends, probably as a result in large measure of the wider range of qualifications brought into the definitions of key targets. However, there was no difference between the two groups overall.

Table 6.8 shows the figures for those securing no grades whatsoever. It suggests that the national averages have seen only modest reductions over the period 2001 to 2005. Octet schools seem to have almost halved the proportions falling into this category over this period. The position appears in the comparison schools to have followed a similar pattern but not to the same extent.

Table 6.8   Proportions of pupils achieving no GCSE grades (or equivalent) in the SFECC and comparison Schools 2001–2005

	National(%)	SFECC(%)	Comparison Schools(%)
2001	5.5	10.1	12.4
2002	5.4	9.9	9.1
2003	5.2	9.6	10.1
2004*	4.1	5.8	10.2
2005**	2.6	5.2	8.1

*From 2004 a wider range of qualifications have been included by the DfES in constructing this indicator. The figures in this table have been weighted to take account of differences in cohort size across the schools.

**The 2005 percentages are for pupils at the end of Key Stage 4, *not* pupils aged 15 as previously.

Source: DfES

We also considered changes in the GCSE/GNVQ Points Scores between the two groups (see Table 6.9). To put the figures for 2004 and 2005 in our time-series we were obliged to recalculate what the results would have been if the old scoring system had been retained. In the absence of more detailed data on individual pupils our figures are, of necessity, approximations.

The initial effects of 'capping' in 2002 on the national averages are clearly evident in this table but, as already suggested, the consequences for both groups of schools appear to have been rather modest, at least by contrast with the changes nationally. In both cases the group averages went down but only by around a fifth of a point on the scale.

Table 6.9   Average GCSE/GNVQ points scores in the SFECC and Comparison Schools 2001–2005

	National	SFECC	Comparison Schools
2001 (uncapped)	39.3	21.4	22.2
2002 (capped)	34.7	21.2	22.0
2003 (capped)	34.8	22.3	22.1
2004* (uncapped)	340*	231*	225*
2004** (uncapped)	?*	24.9*	25.5*
2005* (uncapped)	355	s260	265
2005** (uncapped)	?	28.8*	29.0*

Notes: A point on the scale is equivalent to an improvement of one grade in one subject, for example from a grade E to a grade D or a grade D to a grade C.

  * From 2004 a wider range of qualifications have been included by the DfES in constructing this indicator. The figures in this table have been weighted to take account of differences in cohort size across the schools.

** We have recalculated these figures in an attempt to use the same metric for the 2004 figures as those employed in previous years – they are, of necessity, approximations.

Source: DfES

Broadly speaking, changes in the two groups of schools appear to have mirrored each other, both going up over the period by very similar amounts. In the case of the SFECC schools the changes over the three years of the project appear to have been fairly steady, amounting to somewhere over a grade in a single subject per year from 2001 to 2004 followed by a further increase in 2005. However, these were, to a very large extent, matched in the comparison schools which made equivalent steps.

Finally, we compared the progress of the eight schools and the comparison group in terms of the value-added measures. As already explained, the two groups were initially matched on the basis of estimates we ourselves made from data for 2001 (tables not shown) and the picture seems to have remained the same across the three years of the project. Table 6.10 shows that both groups of schools were, on average, performing each year below national expectations with respect to progress from Key Stage 3 to GCSE. A rather similar (but slightly more pessimistic) picture emerges with respect to Key Stage 2 to GCSE. Furthermore, there were no obvious upward trends in the value-added measures.

Table 6.10   Value-added scores between (a) Key Stage 3 and GCSE and (b) Key Stage 2 and GCSE for the SFECC and Comparison Schools 2002–2005

(a) KS3 to GCSE	National	SFECC	Comparison Schools
2002	Based around 100	96.6	97.2
2003	Based around 100	97.6	98.4
2004	Based around 1000	979	984
2005	Based around 1000	992	995
(b) KS2 to GCSE			
2004	Based around 1000	947	959
2005	Based around 1000	954	964

* From 2004 a wider range of qualifications have been included by the DfES in constructing this indicator.

Source: DfES

Comparing the effects of different policy initiatives

The improvement programme to which the SFECC schools were recruited was one of a number of policy options. Given the generally low levels of attainment of their pupils they might, in other circumstances, have been judged suitable candidates for one of the other policy initiatives targeted at schools in disadvantaged areas such as Special Measures, the Fresh Start or the Academies programme. In this section we compare their improvement with their possible fates had they been enrolled in one or other of these programmes. This is, of course, a hypothetical comparison, premised on the assumption that these schools were not significantly different from others for whom such initiatives have been deemed suitable.

Much of the evidence in Figure 6.2 was originally collated by the National Audit Office (NAO, 2006: 9). It presents the 'before and after' performance of schools participating in three different school improvement programmes to which we have added in the results for the SFECC schools. The comparisons, in the case of the Academies and Fresh Start programme are, it should be noted, with their predecessor schools which may have had a different make-up in terms of intakes until they

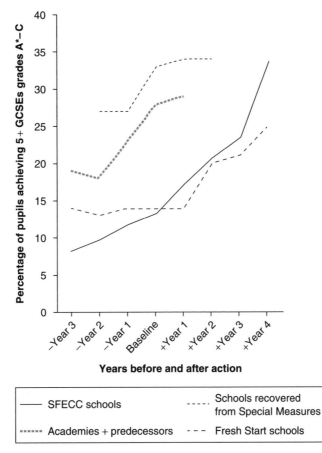

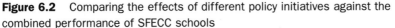

Figure 6.2   Comparing the effects of different policy initiatives against the combined performance of SFECC schools

Source: Developed from data provided in Table 8 in NAO report (2006: 9) on *Improving Poorly Performing Schools in England*.

assumed their new guises. Unfortunately, the comparisons are also limited to just the one outcome measure. It should also be borne in mind that the timings in the figure relate to the phase of each intervention rather than the same calendar years.

The first and most obvious point to be made is that the SFECC programme seems to have been targeted at a group of schools whose initial levels of performance fell some way short of those being addressed by the other programmes. Inspecting Figure 6.2 it is clear that the performance of schools on Special Measures and in the Academies programme was running considerably ahead of those in the SFECC project. How far these provide useful comparators is therefore a moot point.

The group of schools which seem to have been closest to the SFECC group in terms of attainment levels were those engaged in Fresh Starts. Fresh Start schools are initially closed and then re-opened with refurbished facilities and major changes or additions to staffing. Even the Fresh Start schools, however, seem to have started from a higher base than the SFECC group – the percentages of their pupils achieving the 5+ A*–C hurdle were running between 5% and 10% ahead.

As Figure 6.2 suggests, both the SFECC and Fresh Start schools were making at best slow improvements (in the former case) or flat-lining (in the latter) prior to the intervention. In both cases their results began to improve around a year after the intervention had started. Indeed, the two lines representing each group of schools seem to have followed remarkably similar paths. Interestingly, those for schools in Special Measures appear to have flat-lined *after* the intervention whilst, at the time of writing, it is too early to say what the fate of the Academies might be although interestingly they seem to have had their *steepest* rise in performance in the run-up to their recruitment to the programme, rather than in its initial years.

Reaching an overall assessment about changes in measured performance

We started this chapter by asserting that a straightforward judgement could be reached about the overall success of the SFECC initiative. All the schools achieved better exam results in 2005 than they had been securing five years earlier. In two cases the apparent extent of improvement was quite dramatic. However, as we have also argued, just relying on increases in 'raw' results runs the risk of providing an unduly simplistic assessment.

When national results are going up across the board every school needs to improve to some extent simply in order to maintain its position. Consequently we sought evidence for steady improvement in the schools' performance across a number of different indicators. We were especially interested in any evidence of *trends over time* and improvements in the progress pupils made indicated by rising levels of *value-added*. Using these broader criteria would suggest that four of the eight schools made reasonable progress whilst none went backwards.

We tried two different ways of putting this figure of four out of eight schools into some kind of broader context. First, we compared the changes in the SFECC schools' performance as a group with another larger group of schools that were 'similar' in almost all respects. The schools in this comparison group were also under pressure to improve and some of them were in other initiatives. As it turned out, both groups of schools secured year-on-year improvements of three to four percentage points between 2001 and 2005. In the process they were able to narrow the gap between themselves and the national average which, whilst it went up, did not rise so rapidly. However, at the same time, it should be noted both the SFECC and the comparison groups made similar progress. The former did not stand out in any way from the latter.

Our second analysis plotted the progress of the SFECC group against that of other comparable policy initiatives taking place during this period in which, had circumstances been different, the schools might have found themselves. These included the Special Measures programme, the Fresh Start and the Academy initiatives. The advantage of this kind of approach is that it locates the benchmarks for policy development in terms of feasible alternatives rather than some arbitrarily chosen (albeit desirable) expectation.

The evidence suggests that both the Special Measures and Academies enrolled schools whose pupils had considerably higher starting points on average than those in the SFECC initiative. This means that their experiences are unlikely to have been closely comparable. It is clear, nonetheless, that in neither of these two programmes did the participating schools *as a group* improve a great deal, at least in the short term, as a direct result of the initiative.

The most pertinent comparison in terms of prior attainment levels, it turns out, was with the group of Fresh Start schools. As the National Audit Office (2006: 8.19) has noted, in these cases the school is initially closed and then 'replaced with a new school with a new name'. This strategy is reserved for schools 'in the most difficult of circumstances'. The NAO estimated that to set up a Fresh Start school could cost well over £2m. Whilst it was 'the most expensive option for school recovery', they were satisfied that the evidence of improved school achievement was 'particularly good' (NAO, 2006: 8.21). Since the performance of the SFECC schools seems to have tracked that of the Fresh Starts at every point the auditors, we assume, might have reached a similar conclusion about this initiative as well.

Our own view of all the evidence on performance presented in this chapter is more mixed. Some schools made considerable progress, others less so. The constant of such initiatives, we would conclude, is that progress across schools is likely to be variable.

QUESTIONS FOR REFLECTION AND DISCUSSION

1. How appropriate are exam results as the main measure of school improvement for the purposes of school accountability?
2. What other measures should be added to provide a more complete picture of a school's performance? If some of these things can't be measured, does it matter?
3. Should the outcomes and expectations be different for schools serving notably disadvantaged communities from schools serving other types of community?

4. People talk of 'lies, damned lies and statistics'. If different ways of looking at a school's performance appear to give different answers, what conclusions, if any, can usefully be drawn?

5. After three years of improvement many schools appear to come to a halt. What are some of the factors in a school which are likely to need particular priority if progress is to be continued? How many of these are fully under a school's own control?

7

Schools for the Future

This final chapter:

- reflects on the extent to which the SFECC project has shown the way forward for schools on the edge;
- discusses the extent to which it sheds light on issues facing educational policy and practice more broadly and
- contemplates the future of schooling, particularly for children and young people growing up in disadvantaged communities.

The impact of the intervention

The quality of the Octet schools and their improvement journey is told in part by the performance data that we presented in Chapter 6, but beneath those statistics a more complex and multi-layered story can be told. In Chapters 4 and 5 we tried to capture some of the optimism and ambition of these eight schools, hardly warranted by the circumstances in which they found themselves. It was their residual vitality and vision of a better future for young people that led them to enlist and rise to the challenge of the SFECC project.

In Chapter 1 we described three approaches to improvement variously described as tactical, strategic and capacity building. Two of these approaches are reflected in the student performance data which shows a general, if uneven, rise on measured attainment over the period of the SFECC intervention. Interviews with school staff reveal the extent to which, underlying these data, were tactical and strategic measures, impelled by the need to demonstrate improvement but typically accompanied by frustration as to the nature of the 'game' and the opportunity costs it entailed. An equally important indicator of quality and improvement would have been to derive a measure of capacity building, that is the extent to which these schools were now more resilient, more change friendly and more self-confident in reaching out to their local communities. In many respects, all or some of the Octet schools would meet such criteria but with differing developmental profiles. To have obtained such a systematic picture during our fieldwork, however, would have required a much fuller commitment than these schools were willing (or able) to make.

What is clear is that the schools differed in the extent to which they embraced the various elements of the programme. As we showed in Chapter 5, some of these, such as the development of a School Improvement Group, were taken up enthusiastically by all of the Octet schools; others, notably the RML reading programme, were explored by only a few, with some of the schools ignoring them completely. Another reason for caution is the lack of a clear correlation between the extent of take-up of elements of the SFECC intervention and the emerging performance of each school. The two schools that could be said to have embraced the project most fully, Campion and The Ridings, were by the end of project, the two schools in which student attainment had improved least. By contrast, the school which had engaged least with the project, Phoenix, had the most improved attainment scores. This is not to argue for a negative correlation, rather that the improvement equation is a complex one. Schools improved by virtue of what was already in place and could be built on, by the ways in which the SFECC project was used to complement and enhance existing initiatives, and by the critical contribution of a full staffing complement.

A key assumption underpinning the selection of the schools for inclusion in the project was that they had good leadership so that, with this as a given, the project could then test other factors that might contribute to overcoming exceptionally challenging circumstances. This was, however, a highly problematic assumption. It was premised on the capacity of eight individuals to effect radical change in very volatile circumstances. In the event only four of the heads who signed up are now still in the same school. In highly stressful situations, with pressures of targets, constant HMI attention and media spotlight, the health of hard-pressed individuals could not be taken for granted. The energy needed to lead such schools proved not to be annually renewable, nor could it be assumed that effective leaders would not be sought after elsewhere.

A useful contribution would be to identify a correlation (and preferably a strong and causal link) between improved pupil performance and leadership style, but this has proved an elusive goal for researchers for many years, since pupil performance is mediated by so many other factors (see for example Mulford, 2003). What can be said with some degree of confidence, however, is that successful leaders help to create conditions in which teachers' commitment is enhanced and in which pupils' learning flourishes. What also seems clear is that a more distributed approach to leadership has enhanced the ownership and initiative of staff beyond those with formal status or position, exemplified most obviously in the vitality of the School Improvement Groups (SIGs).

Among the various elements of the SFECC initiative it was these SIGs that were most widely welcomed and seen as a key lever of change. For a SIG to have an impact, however, demands a stability, sustainability and capacity within the school. As many of the heads and teachers in the eight schools agreed, the single most important precondition of improvement was a full complement of staffing, with a healthy balance of expertise. This is simply what any good school would take for granted. To conclude that schools in exceptionally challenging circumstances simply require additional support and resourcing does not address the more fundamental question: what are the critical factors that need to be in place to enable *all* young people to gain access to a genuinely fulfilling educational experience?

The pursuit of 'education for all'

To understand the future or the present it is necessary to have some understanding of the past. Education for all is today an uncontested value and schooling is widely accepted as the means to that end. However, less than a century and a half ago, mass schooling was seen as a threat to the established order. Robert Lowe, in an effort to assuage anxious members of the House of Commons, has been famously quoted as saying: 'If it is not cheap, it shall be efficient; if it is not efficient, it shall be cheap.' (Hansard, 1867: 1546). It was a reluctant state that brought in basic schooling for all, partly out of meagre charity and partly to be able to hold some sway over the voters enfranchised by the Reform Act of 1867. While schooling for all was achieved in Britain in the nineteenth century, a few years into the twenty-first we are still not able to claim that schools as we know them are able to offer a fulfilling education for *all* our children.

It is a problem acknowledged by the present government, one prepared to adventure with new forms of schooling and, with the help of private enterprise, to invest in state-of-the-art academies to replace struggling schools. The Building Schools for the Future (BSF) programme has been described as 'the largest capital investment programme since the Second World War' (Kelly, 2006). The 2003 consultation paper report which illustrated many of the DfES's 'exemplar designs' would, it claimed, promote community involvement, be a good place for children to learn and teachers to teach, supported by ICT, and 'drive reform of the secondary system and improvement in educational standards' (DfES, 2003: 3).

Even before they have had a chance to settle in, academies have been pronounced an unqualified success by the DfES:

Academies are now addressing entrenched school failure in our most deprived areas and are starting to transform educational opportunity for thousands of our

young people who need it most. The first 27 Academies are up and running and
we are already seeing significant improvements in results in these communities,
with results in Academies rising more than three times as fast as the national
average between 2004 and 2005. (DfES, 2005b: 15)

By foregrounding the need for academies, however, the potential contribution of
other 'bog standard' schools to the agenda is inevitably downgraded. Other
voices have sounded a greater note of caution. The Government Select
Committee, which reported in March 2005, concluded that there was as yet
little evidence to justify the cost of academies of £21,000 per pupil, as against
£14,000 for a new comprehensive school. They found no 'overarching strategy',
no independent evidence to justify the cost and pointed out that of the first
eleven academies five had not improved and some had got worse, one had been
put into Special Measures in 2005 (House of Commons Select Committee, 2005).
A study by Wrigley (*Guardian*, 2006) which compared results from the first
eleven academies with the schools they had replaced, found an increase in GCSE
grades (5 A*–C) of just 0.02%. The government's determination to live with the
rough and the smooth of educational innovation, in the cause of seeking to
address educational disadvantage, needs to be extended to other schools not able
to mobilise the resources required for complete renewal.

William Atkinson, head of Phoenix, one of the most successful of the Octet
schools, does not believe that academies are the answer for schools like his.
Schools whose classrooms are filled with the most challenging students, he
argues in an article in the *Guardian*, need a modern day 'Marshall Plan'
(Atkinson, 2006; see Figure 7.1). Much of what he proposed dated back to his
original proposal for a project such as SFECC, where he argued that only with a
sound infrastructure of resourcing and support could a school such as his build
bridges between in-school and out-of-school learning and help to regenerate
communities on the edge.

William Atkinson's 'Marshall Plan' is centred on the needs of the children and, where possible, their
local community. The essential elements of the plan are:

- class sizes of fewer than 20 students;
- full-time, permanent teachers judged to be good or better;
- continuing professional development;
- extensive range of extra-curricular activities;
- involvement of professionals other than teachers, such as social workers, counsellors and
  educational psychologists;
- parental engagement and family learning;
- good physical environment;
- good resource level.

Figure 7.1 A Marshall Plan for schools on the edge
Source: Atkinson (2006)

According to a recent audit by the NFER, there has been 'a quiet revolution' in this area. Provision under this banner includes extra-curricular activities, community facilities such as advice centres, pre-school facilities, crèches, parent support and provision by other agencies working from the school site (Wilkin et al., 2003). The government has said it is keen to encourage the development of extended schooling, and enterprising headteachers have seen in this opportunities for enhanced funding and renewed vision. In 2004, the Minister for Extended and Inclusive Schools said that she wanted:

> *... to encourage every school to provide extended services and we have changed the law to make it easier for them to do this. We are also providing guidance, support and funding for every LEA to help all their schools to develop the services most needed by their community.* (Ashton, 2004)

The wellsprings of this 'quiet revolution' are in the 'full service' school movement in the United States (Dryfoos, 1994), imported into Scotland as 'new community schools' in 1998, and as extended schools in England in 2002 (Dryfoos et al., 2005). The concept of 'full service' is a recognition of the fact that schools can only offer a partial service and that learning is not simply a product of teaching but is acutely dependent on mental and physical health, diet, emotional stability and the quality of relationships in school, home and community. Educationists and governments have long espoused the education of 'the whole child' but, as the whole child lives in so many different social contexts, 'full service' requires a concerted effort to bring services to children and families into closer alignment. The one door entry to all social, health and educational services is the 'big idea' of the full service school.

In Scotland, the Executive have seen further than the 'new community' or 'extended' school, to envision community learning and community development as intrinsic elements of any attempt to deal with the challenges of circumstance.

> *Community learning and development describes a way of working with and supporting communities. We see community learning and development as central to 'social capital' – a way of working with communities to increase the skills, confidence, networks and resources they need to tackle problems and grasp opportunities. We want community learning and development to bring together the best of what has been done under the banners of 'community education' and 'community development' to help individuals and communities tackle real issues in their lives through community action and community-based learning.* (Scottish Executive, 2004)

An evaluation of the initiative shows that it had some teeth and was making progress; 'a cocktail of approaches' linked by the New Community School (NCS) concept could act 'as a catalyst for change and innovation, and increased multi-agency approaches, professional development and communication were evident'. (Sammons et al., 2003: 3) As we found in this study, however, whilst attainment levels rose in NCS schools they did so in other schools as well (Sammons et al., 2003). Clearly it is what such extended schools can offer over and above the conventional outcomes that demands deeper exploration.

Some might claim an earlier ancestry for the concept. Cambridgeshire Village Colleges, conceived of by Henry Morris, provided a bold vision for ridding schooling of the dualities of 'education and ordinary life' and 'the dismal dispute of the vocational and non-vocational'. The village colleges were to serve the most disadvantaged communities, to provide for the whole person and not to be just the training ground for the art of living, but the place in which life is lived. Education was not to be seen as something that took place solely in the classroom. It was described in these idyllic terms:

> *The village college as thus outlined would not create something superfluous; it would not be a spectacular experiment and a costly luxury. It would take all the various vital but isolated activities in village life – the School, the Village Hall and Reading Room, the Evening Classes, the Agricultural Education Courses, the Women's Institute, the British Legion, Boy Scouts and Girl Guides, the recreation ground, the branch of the County Rural Library, the Athletic and Recreation Clubs – and, bringing them together into relation, create a new institution for the English countryside. It would create out of discrete elements an organic whole.* (Morris, 1925: Section XIV)

The village college was to be a visible demonstration of education 'from the cradle to the grave' – the 'never ceasingness' of education. In Morris's vision the school leaving age would become a misnomer because school would only be the beginning of a commitment to lifelong learning.

While Morris's bold vision was only realised in part, and the existing village colleges are a remaining tribute to his genius, it is only three quarters of a century on that his idea is being given tangible expression, not only in the UK but in countries around the world in which new forms of community outreach are emerging. In São Paulo in Brazil, for example, the UNESCO backed Escola de Familia programme is a radical solution to communities with escalating levels of street crime, where high schools were regularly wrecked during periods when they were closed. The situation has been radically transformed by establishing a system where schools are occupied almost round the clock every day of the year. Members of the community come into school in order to learn from each other. They offer whatever skills they have and take courses in everything from cookery to working in call-centres. University students also provide tuition in return for their own tuition fees (www.escoladafamilia.sp.gov.br).

The 24 hour school, once regarded as an outlandish notion, is now closer to being realised. In the global information age, in which India is at work in our down-time and in which the conventional eight hour day does not apply to many professions or to the way young people live their lives, a resource open to the community around the clock can start to cater to a range of needs and interests. Resources which would otherwise lie idle through evenings, weekends and holiday periods can be put to the service of a whole community.

This is one model of a new 'comprehensive' school, drawing people of all ages into one central campus, an all-embracing community resource. There is another, different kind of model, however, one which works in the opposite direction, pushing provision out to local neighbourhoods, creating smaller scale, more easily accessible and more convivial locations. The concept of 'street academies' which flourished in the 1970s in the United States, was based on the accessibility of local small units such as storefront learning centres sited on main thorough-fares or in shopping malls. Versions of this can be seen in most cities in the form of Internet cafés, libraries as community learning resources, tutorial agencies, and complementary provision as in Kumon learning centres which are growing at a prodigious rate in the UK. (There are now 550 such centres across the country. www.kumon.co.uk/findcentre/)

New Philanthropy Capital, a company which advises investors on the viability of city academies, suggested in 2006 that money would be better spent on smaller local initiatives such as breakfast clubs and study support. It urged potential donors to consider alternatives such as sponsoring breakfast clubs or out-of-hours clubs aimed at helping youngsters struggling to learn to read or write. It points out that for £2m a sponsor could support after school clubs for 10,000 children. Alternatively, if a sponsor were to donate the money to an anti-bullying charity such as Kidscape or ChildLine, for example, it could pay for training 2,000 teachers in how to tackle bullying – potentially benefiting 60,000 children (Garner, 2006).

There is a plethora of local initiatives which already exist in parallel with extended schools, many unbeknown to their local schools. There are clearly benefits to be gained from a more co-ordinated approach. Community-based centres could function as networked satellites, providing access to school resources on a virtual basis as well as benefiting from more hands-on expertise of school personnel taken out to local learning centres.

Promising technologies

The SFECC project only scratched the surface of what new technologies could offer to young people, to teachers and to the wider community. Much of the project's early promise of inter-school networking and user-friendly interfaces was not realised, although the transformative potential of ICT was widely recognised and anticipated. Interactive whiteboards did come to fruition and extended the compass of the classroom. The novelty of the medium, when well deployed, proved a motivating factor for pupils, encouraging them to pose and pursue questions in the flow of the lesson, capturing and instantly displaying their contribution to building and exchanging knowledge, as Wall et al. (2005) have commented on elsewhere. The creative use of interactive whiteboards clearly added value to the 'delivery' of a lesson, yet there was little evidence in Octet schools of this resource playing a more dynamic role, putting the technology much more into the hands of young people and enabling them to have a stronger voice in their own learning (Good, 2006). The failure to extend the role of this and other interactive technologies was not because teachers lacked imagination, but because the tight constraints of timetabling and curriculum coverage fragmented learning and teaching and worked at cross purposes to coherent understanding.

While many young people in these eight schools were disengaged from formal classroom learning, nonetheless they exhibited a sophisticated command of a range of information technologies, including facility with mobile phones, texting, video games, blogging, podcasting, as well as a discriminating knowledge of websites. The immense popularity of myspace.com, for example, indicates the levels of motivation and ability among young people to participate in the global communication network.

The potential of children and young people to acquire technological skills in a short space of time without teaching or adult intervention was demonstrated in a remarkable series of experiments in India with slum children (Mitra and Rana, 2001). Untutored children, who had never seen a computer before, were given access to hole in the wall computers in their villages and, when tested on the self-taught skills they had acquired, performed just as well as, indeed slightly better than, their counterparts who had been taught computing skills in school over an extended period (Imamdar, 2004).

The gains were not simply to individual children but distributed through social networks. A sociometric survey carried out to examine how this took place found patterns of knowledge flow, social networking, self-regulation and collaboration (www.hole-in-the-wall.com/Findings.html). The study found 'self-organising' groups of children capable of distinguishing their various levels of expertise, able to connect and teach others and with an unexpectedly prominent lead taken by girls in inducting others. While these children performed slightly less well on the theory part of tests they were given, the fact that they were able to theorise to a relatively high standard on the basis of experience and social networking alone, was confirmation of a stream of influential ideas that go back to John Dewey and beyond.

What these studies showed is that we vastly underestimate the hidden skills and motivation of children, which we rarely get a glimpse of because we persist in measuring them against preconceived sets of standards and benchmarks. Recognising the capacity of children to problem solve, to explore the ether and make connections is not an argument for a laissez-faire, hands-off approach but rather for a form of scaffolding which both validates and challenges informal and intuitive learning:

> *The growth of connections, both in number and diversity, poses a challenge. If they are to be useful and not threatening, supporting understanding rather than confusion, harmony rather than cacophony, we must learn to use them to create valued relationships.* (Bentley, 1998: 158)

Where the future challenges lie

The challenges for the future are the nature and quality of learning experiences, the structures which contain them and the belief systems which hold them in place. In 1981, Simon published 'Why no pedagogy in England?' Thirty years later Alexander followed this with his own rhetorical question 'Still no Pedagogy?' With reference to the government's espousal of both excellence and enjoyment he writes:

> *Excellence and Enjoyment relies heavily on large print, homely language, images of smiling children, and populist appeals to teachers' common sense. Substantively, it seeks to secure professional goodwill, and possibly to disarm criticism, by relaxing the pressure of government prescription and targets. But beyond this surface appeal are important statements on learning, teaching, curriculum and assessment, which are arguably the core of that pedagogy whose absence Brian Simon deplored.* (Alexander, 2004: 1)

As we have consistently argued in the preceding pages, young people need to experience a curriculum in which they recognise themselves, one which allows them to develop a sense of their own agency, a principle that is writ large in disadvantaged communities.

The evaluation of the SFECC initiative exposes a lack of pedagogy, a deficit concealed by the 'surface appeal' of policies imbued with more rhetoric than substance. In the mid-nineteenth century Herbert Spencer put forward a proposal which would go beyond the narrow confines of subject-based learning and even beyond the idea of work-related learning.

> *How to live? – that is the essential question ... in what way to treat the body .... the mind. To manage our affairs .... To bring up a family ... to behave as a citizen .... To utilize those resources for happiness that nature supplies .... how to live completely .... To prepare us for complete living is the function which education has to discharge.* (Spencer, 1861: 6)

In what way is 'complete living' enhanced by the curriculum diet which we currently offer to the young? Many of the gains made in the 1960s and 70s in respect of 'creativity', 'open learning', 'critical thinking', 'inquiry-based learning' and so on, melted away with the pressure for 'coverage' of the National Curriculum. Innovations in social studies, integrated humanities and the like were developed in response to the raising of the school leaving age as well as through the reasoning of philosophers of education such as Paul Hirst, and through the deliberations of HMI. Under the Thatcher government 'progressive' ideas were killed off in a 'discourse of derision' (Wallace, 1993 after Ball, 1990), to be replaced by a curriculum based on a diet of school subjects, one that would have been familiar to pupils attending grammar schools half a century or more ago. According to Goodson, these abandoned innovations had constituted a challenge to the 'hegemony of the grammar school curriculum' and were therefore not included in the reforms driven by a perceived crisis in national identity (1994: 103). The subject-based curriculum is one that alienates students who do not recognise themselves or their culture reflected in what they are being offered (Weiss and Fine, 2000). Some critics go as far as to say that such a curriculum is often 'disrespectful' (Apple, 2006). Mortimore (2006) suggests an eight stage improvement strategy to redress the situation, drawing on the NUT visionary paper *Bringing Down the Barriers* (2005: 50–5):

- dismantling the 'pecking order' of schools;
- rescinding the market forces approach to school choice;
- reviewing the national curriculum;
- rethinking the national assessment system;
- creating new pedagogies;
- enhancing current models of teacher training;
- remodelling the inspection arrangements;
- creating a standing body to deliberate on educational changes.

School effectiveness researchers have argued with some validity that progressivist ideas worked to the advantage of middle class pupils who were more comfortable with looser structures and greater independence. Nevertheless, it is evident from the SFECC project that, however popular the three/four part lesson, and the added attraction of whiteboard technology, the transmission model is alive and well but leaves many children intellectually and emotionally adrift.

The dilemma is that, although a subject-based curriculum may well have the effect of disenfranchising some young people, gaining credentials remains the passport to economic and social success. In a world of stratified knowledge where some forms of knowing have more cachet than others, it may be argued that it does young people no favours to increase enjoyment and engagement while failing to lead them beyond their limited aspirations. However, if the content of the curriculum results in disaffection, with little or no authentic learning taking place, then the question of the status of knowledge acquired becomes redundant. The former Secretary of State for Education, Ruth Kelly, set out proposals in the 14–19 White Paper (DfES, 2005a) in which she foregrounded the aim to 're-engage the disaffected'. However, although the amount of prescription in the Key Stage 4 curriculum was reduced in 2004, there was little in that document to suggest support for the sort of innovations which might make a difference in 'exceptionally challenging circumstances'.

The opportunity offered by the Tomlinson Review (DfES, 2004) had been missed. The government rejected its major recommendations for reform and principally the proposal that GCSE and A Level should be replaced by a coherent framework of qualifications for the 14–19 age group, with an 'interlocking' curriculum across each level, providing the basis for cumulative progression from one level to the next. Tomlinson also proposed radical changes in which particular qualifications would be taken with a view to bridging the present day pre-16/post-16 barrier with, for example, the possibility of vertical groupings and shifts in specialism. The proposal for functional ICT as a basic necessary skill, to be formally recognised alongside mathematics and English could have given overdue recognition to facility in ICT (including all the associated expertise in media applications, graphic art and design and digital technology) as a more appealing route out of poverty than formal academic qualifications.

The Foster Review (2005) meanwhile found a continuing belittling of the Further Education sector, the poor child of the education system. Yet Further Education colleges contribute more than a third of all entrants to higher education and are the main route for adults and entrants from lower socio-economic groups.

There is a widely shared concern that due to their cultural background large numbers of pupils are disenfranchised by the lack of suitable pathways. These pupils are also disadvantaged by a lack of recognition that consistently used teaching strategies may not suit predispositions to ways of learning or learning preferences. Notwithstanding critiques of the reliability of the tools and techniques for identifying learning preferences (Coffield et al., 2004), there is evidence from the SFECC project, from Frost (2005) and from the Coffield study itself, that paying attention to learning preferences can enhance pupils' achievements. In practice, however, it tends to be seen as a way of getting a better toehold on the curriculum rather than following through on the more radical implications of where an understanding of 'styles' and 'preferences' might lead.

The contention that pupils are more likely to commit themselves to learning if their differences are recognised, resonates well with the government's 'personalisation' campaign. But what this means has never been fully explained and it appears to be left to teachers, senior leaders and researchers (Mortimore, 2006) to try and invest the concept with real meaning. It remains to be seen if personalisation can move beyond the limiting and deterministic notion of meeting curricular targets and encourage us to think differently about how pupils can develop their own sense of agency.

There is one further dimension that the schools like those in the SFECC project will need help to embrace more fully – namely the power of 'pupil voice' as a means to change. As Rudduck and Flutter remark: '[its] transformative potential relates closely to the development of a stronger sense of the school as an inclusive community' (2004: 152). Ranson (2000) also talks of the power of voice in the remaking of communities, a means through which young people can engage with others in transforming practice. Such ambitions were precisely what the Octet were struggling to achieve, and while there was evidence of schools paying closer attention to the voice of their students it was not a major plank of the SFECC intervention, particularly in relation to the building of bridges into the community. It takes not only determination but acutely tuned antennae to hear the voice of the marginalised in marginalised communities.

A question of structure

Personalising learning will be an empty gesture without radical rethinking of the structures which contain it. In the early 1970s Ivan Illich delivered a seismic shock to the system with his proposals for deschooling society (Illich, 1970). It was a call for a complete dismantling of school structures because, he argued, they were anti-educational. The implications of Illich's ideas for wide school reform were too sweeping to give serious thought to but he did expose a deep structural fault line in the system which, he argued, was inhibiting of human agency. Echoing Basil Bernstein's famous dictum, Anyon in the US comments that 'educational reforms cannot compensate for the ravages of society' because:

> *The structural basis for failure in inner-city schools is political, economic and cultural, and must be changed before meaningful school improvement projects can be successfully implemented.* (Anyon quoted in Berliner, 2005: 6)

A system in which schools are devolved, self-improving units in competition with one another in this deeply divided society has created a sense of embattlement. This is further intensified by the government promise to get tougher with failing schools (DfES, 2005b) rather than, as happens in more enlightened regimes, to work closely and supportively with schools in difficulty (see for example, Mortimore, 2006: 43–4). As Smith has argued, the insularity and 'fiefdom' mentality which governs schools prevents them from collaborating with their closest neighbours, and deters the building of bridges with other agencies or increasing traffic among different sites and sources of expertise with disastrous consequences:

> *Things have tended to be done on [the schools'] terms or not at all. Collaboration in community education initiatives has often been possible in the past because they were relatively insulated from what principals and heads saw as the 'main' activities of the school.* (Smith, 2005)

It was not only the 'main activities of the school' to which Illich and other fellow travellers drew attention, but what they saw as the invisible message of the 'hidden curriculum'. To focus on the content of the curriculum was, critics argued, to miss the deeper, more insidious issue – the process by which learning and teaching were engaged, and the underpinning belief system which filtered day by day into habits and dispositions. In Marshall McLuhan's words 'the medium is the message' (1967). In other words, it is less the content of the curriculum than the medium through which it is 'delivered' that denies the sense of human agency.

Radical solutions require courageous and determined action at a local level within a national framework which encourages adventurous innovation, which is prepared to acknowledge that government doesn't know it all, which is able to admit that, in some critical respects, it has got things wrong. There is perhaps a glimmer of hope in the QCA's recent document *The Curriculum: QCA Looks Forward* which promises that the QCA will act strategically over the next three years to support innovation at the local level. 'We intend', they write, 'to support schools and communities in their own efforts to design and implement the curriculum'; and later they comment that their aim is 'to create a climate where people think creatively and innovatively about how the curriculum can provide the best learning experience for young people' (QCA, 2006: 3).

While this statement may be music to the ears of those who have argued against centrally-driven, national reforms as stultifying, it has to be remembered that the QCA document was produced against the backdrop of a deeply entrenched culture of high stakes testing and bureaucratic accountability, one that has succeeded in keeping the wellsprings of creativity and innovation firmly capped. Local development of a curriculum that is genuinely responsive to the needs of young people on the edge of society requires leadership that is courageous, resilient and relentlessly learning-focused. Since 2004 headteachers have been encouraged in this by the publication of the revised professional standards for headteachers which includes a section headed 'Strengthening Community'. The document makes the following declaration.

Schools exist in a distinctive social context, which has a direct impact on what happens inside the school. School leadership should commit to engaging with the internal and external school community to secure equity and entitlement. Headteachers should collaborate with other schools in order to share expertise and bring positive benefits to their own and other schools. They should work collaboratively at both strategic and operational levels with parents and carers and across multiple agencies for the well-being of all children. Headteachers share responsibility for leadership of the wider educational system and should be aware that school improvement and community development are interdependent. (DfES, 2004b: 11)

In communities where social capital is low, the above statement may need a stronger interpretation. If headteachers 'share responsibility for the leadership of the wider educational system', this implies that leadership in disadvantaged communities needs to be about a sharing of responsibility for the community itself. A pilot 'Developing Community Leadership Programme' sponsored by the National College for School Leadership brings headteachers together with other community leaders to explore their practice and give meaning to concepts such as 'social entrepreneurship'. The report of the pilot (Mckenley, 2005) celebrates the progress made by the participants who were working within an action learning framework. More substantial research and trialling is needed, however, to make visible the way that community leadership may impact on education, social capital and economic regeneration.

Community leadership does not imply heroic headship. Indeed any muscular high profile approach is likely to be highly counter-productive in a context in which it is wise to tread softly. This is an area in which the concept of 'distributed leadership' can be made genuinely meaningful through the building of alliances and supportive networks. This is a challenging goal, not just because education professionals may be unwilling to expose themselves to this extent, but because of the difficulty in defining what constitutes the 'community' served by the school.

Mortimore concludes that successful change cannot be achieved through legislation or top-down command but through dialogue within schools and between schools and their communities. He writes:

> There is a difference in being expected to implement what has been decided by other people and being enabled to contribute to the debate about the nature of possible change. (2006: 56)

One of the central failings of the SFECC project was its top-down approach to change, where the opportunities existed for a much more collaborative bottom-up approach. Nonetheless, the high and low points, the successes and failures experienced by the SFECC schools, offer some salutary lessons for policy-making.

Nine lessons for policy makers

We have resisted the temptation to say that the SFECC project did or didn't 'work'. Some of its elements proved highly successful. Others were something of a failure. Our ultimate concern lies with the conception of an intervention that was too narrowly and inwardly focused, too impatient to be able to get to grips with nature of the challenging circumstances themselves. One of the burdens the schools who signed up for it had to endure was that they ran the risk of becoming victims of expectations that were, on the one hand, overly-ambitious, and, on the other, too short sighted.

One of the conclusions to emerge from this study reinforces our suspicion that the circumstances of schools on the edge have been under-researched. The National Commission on Education's study of 'success against the odds' celebrated some of the 'successes' whilst reflecting on the extent to which even these 'beacons of hope' were having difficulty sustaining their achievements (Maden, 2001); however, it made no pretence of being representative of schools in disadvantaged areas. In setting up the SFECC project the DfES chose schools with an eye to demonstrating 'improvements' in two ways. First, by selecting schools where the heads looked as if they were capable of initiating and developing changes. And second, by getting external experts to assess their 'readiness for change'. Weighting the dice in this way strikes us as a sensible precaution but it does mean that the conclusions generated here are only generalisable to schools in similar positions. For insights into what might have happened in a random sample of schools on the edge one must, for the present, turn to the measured prose of Ofsted reports which, notwithstanding their tendency to stack up debits on such schools' accounts, speaks volumes about the immense size of the challenge facing policy-makers and practitioners.

Much of what happened during the life of the project was, in reality, not that distinctive nor was it unique to the eight schools. As we have shown in Chapter 4 many exciting things were already happening in these schools, so that their response to the relevance and expectations of the project were therefore different. Had the project started from where the schools were, rather than from its own menu of interventions, SFECC would have had been constructed differently and might have had a quite different kind of impact. What the project did achieve was to provide a catalyst for schools to review their existing practice, and to test new ways of working. In this concluding section we attempt to tease out some of the broader lessons.

1. Intervening in schools on the edge is a long-term proposition. Judged in terms of conventional criteria, the investment is risky, and the failure rates historically have been high – higher perhaps than policy-makers are aware of, or care to admit. Furthermore, dividends are slow to emerge. Almost all schools on the edge require considerable and sustained investment.

2. There are systemic reasons why some schools are on the edge. These are not easily addressed by purely *educational* interventions. They require more joined-up social and economic policy. *Every Child Matters* goes some way to recognising the need for more coherent delivery of services but is obliged to work within local infrastructures which do not address wider systemic issues.

3. The longer a school has been floundering, the longer it will usually take to get back on its feet. As a rule of thumb, if the period of difficulties stretches back ten years, it is likely to take five to get back on track and perhaps seven to be

confident of longer-term success. Five years is seen by politicians as a long-term horizon; on the other hand children have to take five years to get through either the primary or secondary stages of schooling. We should be cautious about collapsing time.

4. There are few easy generalisations to be made about the contexts and challenges facing schools on the edge – each school is likely to experience different and occasionally unique problems. Lumping them together and attempting to prescribe common remedies is unlikely to be helpful.

5. The fight for some semblance of stability has to be accepted as a never-ending struggle. The mind-set of many of the key participants in schools on the edge (whether they be school leaders, teachers or pupils) is that of 'temporary residents' – in due course they will move on, perhaps sooner rather than later. 'Fail-safes' need to be built into planning, and resourcing will always be more demanding and expensive than in schools where stability can simply be taken for granted.

6. Few schools are adept at introducing and managing innovations successfully. This capacity is massively under-developed in schools on the edge. However unpalatable, the key lesson for policy-makers is that change takes time to plan and implement, and the stage at which most projects end or wind down is often precisely the point at which the feasibility of potential investments can begin to be assessed – possibly for the first time. Demanding that these same schools simultaneously respond to the short-term pressures imposed by performance tables and Ofsted monitoring can produce the institutional equivalent of schizophrenia. The main legacy in schools on the edge of the 'show-quick-results-at-any-cost' mentality has been a series of failed investments, each in turn adding to the view that 'it might work elsewhere but it won't work here'.

7. Seeking to prescribe the 'what and how' of school improvement in widely differing institutions and social contexts can be counter-productive. Change starts to take root in schools when the staff collectively begin to get hold of a 'powerful idea'. That idea can take a variety of different forms. Policy-makers need to become more adept at drawing up menus of the most promising ideas which schools may approach as 'à la carte', while ordering 'off-menu' should be also examined and appraised on its merits.

8. Taking a broader view of leadership is essential. A 'charismatic' or 'heroic' head-teacher may, in certain circumstances, be needed but the risk is that the template for leadership can be drawn too narrowly, and may in the longer term prove counter-productive. In this respect the setting up of a School Improvement Group (SIG) is significant in distributing leadership. It can create space for teacher leadership and team leadership to emerge and contribute to teacher-led improvement.

9. School improvement groups take a variety of forms but tend to be composed entirely of teaching staff focused on professional development, learning and teaching and school-based issues. If they are to have a wider impact their membership would need to be enhanced by including other people with a broader community perspective. Whatever their constitution, however, the biggest challenge is to take young people's views about teaching, learning and their connectedness to their lives, both in and out of school, more seriously.

A society that is committed to offering all its citizens equal opportunities has no choice about whether to have policies for schools in 'exceptionally challenging circumstances'. Stated baldly, the gap between schools serving mainstream communities and those on the edge is not just large but, in most people's view, unacceptably so. The moral case for intervention should be taken as read, but whatever action is launched in the name of social justice, it should be approached with sensitivity, support and receptiveness to research, combined with a firm grasp on the lessons of history.

QUESTIONS FOR REFLECTION AND DISCUSSION

1. What obstacles to 'education for all' do you perceive?
2. To what extent can the development of full service schooling help to overcome social and economic disadvantage? What can schools do to mobilise the resources within the community they serve so as to maximise the life chances of young people?
3. What do you understand by 'personalised learning'? Does the personalisation agenda give rise to optimism about the possibility of freeing up the curriculum and enabling schools and teachers to be innovative and risk taking?
4. In what ways can new technologies be harnessed to develop a pedagogy that is 'personalised' in ways that meet the needs of young people?
5. What radical solutions would you propose to address the needs and challenges of schools on the edge?

Appendix

Research Methods

The evaluation of the DfES School Facing Exceptionally Challenging Circumstances Project was conducted by a team from the Faculty of Education, University of Cambridge, between April 2002 and March 2005. Both quantitative and qualitative methods were used in the research. The quantitative research included analysis of changes in examination performance in the eight schools over the years 2001–2004, and comparisons over the same time period with a group of similar schools. The qualitative research analysed the effects of the project in each of the schools, changes in the eight schools over the 2–3 years of the project, and the interaction between each of these schools with the community which it serves. In addition, as the SFECC Project was directly organised by the DfES, research into the background and genesis of the project was conducted at the DfES itself using source material, and interviews were also carried out at specific stages of the project with key members of the DfES team. This primary research in the schools was complemented by secondary research on the HMI visits made during the three years of the project, on other evaluation visits made to the schools (for example by Ofsted) on the attitudes of staff and students in the schools reported through the NFER survey commissioned for the project.

There was a timetable of seven major research visits to each school over the course of the project. Extended visits of 1 or 2 days were made each time, involving a mixed data gathering programme of interview, focus group discussion, shadowing and classroom observation with both staff and students. As part of the research into the 'community effects' on the school, interviews were also carried out with school governors, headteachers of feeder primary schools, local community workers and youth project workers. Besides research conducted at the eight schools, the evaluation also covered the staff development programmes organised and funded as part of the SFECC Project, and members of the Cambridge team sat in on the reading programme training, the data management training, the middle management training and the whiteboard training. A researcher observed the majority of all the SIG training conducted over the two year 'implementation phase' of the project.

The evaluation began with a baseline picture of where the schools were in April 2002 with some retrospective account of how far they appeared to have travelled since their first introduction to the project. An important constituent of the baseline was the data on student attainment for the baseline year of 2001, and baseline data on student and staff attitudes from which value-added measures, trajectories of improvement (plateauing and regression) could be derived. Staff attitudes and parental data (for example from the NfER survey) were part of these baseline measures and provided not only a data source but a starting point for individual and group interviews in the schools. Attainment data also provided a useful point of reference for discussions on the meaning, perceived utility, and use of the data at various levels within the school.

The research has produced:

- a set of single site case studies,
- a series of significant comparisons across the 8 schools: of similarities and differences in the ways in which the project took root,
- cross-cutting generalised themes which are significant for policy.

A Final Report on the evaluation was submitted to the DfES in July 2005.

References

Adnet, N. and Davies, P. (2005) 'Competition between or within schools? Re-assessing school choice', *Education Economics*, 13(1), pp. 109–21.

Alexander, R. J. (2004) 'Still no pedagogy? Principle, pragmatism and compliance in primary education', *Cambridge Journal of Education*, 34(1), pp. 7–33.

Alterman, E. (2005) When Presidents Lie, *The Nation*, 25 October.

Apple, M. (2006) *Markets, Standards, and Inequality – Keynote Address to ICSEI* (International Congress on School Effectiveness and Improvement), Fort Lauderdale, Florida, USA. Audio recording retrieved 10 March 2006 from www.leadership.fau.edu/icsei2006/archive.htm.

Arnold, M. (1869) *Culture and Anarchy*, London: Smith, Elder & Co.

Ashton, A. (2004) 'More schools providing community services', *Department for Education and Skills Press Notice*, www.dfes.gov.uk/pns/DisplayPN.cgi?pn_id=2004_0110.

Atkinson, W. (2006) 'A loss of courage, will and faith', *Guardian*, 17 January 2006.

Ball, S. (1990) *Politics and Policy Making in Education: Explorations in Policy Sociology*, London: Routledge.

Ball, S. (2001) Labour, learning and the economy: a 'policy sociology', perspective, in M. Fielding (ed.) *Taking education really seriously, four years hard labour*, London: Falmer Routledge.

Barber, M. (1996) 'Creating a Framework for Success in Urban Areas', in M. Barber and R. Dann (eds), *Raising Educational Standards in the Inner Cities*, London: Cassell.

Bastiani J. (ed.) (1987) *Parents and teachers: Perspectives on home–school relations*, London: NFER Nelson.

Bentley, T. (1998) *Learning Beyond the Classroom*, London: DEMOS

Berliner, D. (2005) 'Our Impoverished View of Educational Reform', *Teachers College Record*, 2 August.

Berliner, D. (2006) Respondent to M. Galton and J. MacBeath, seminar: 'The Lives of Teachers, American Educational Research Association', San Francisco, 9 April.

Bernstein, B. (1970) 'Education cannot compensate for society', *New Society*, 387: 344–7.

Brewer, M., Goodman, A., Shaw, J., Shepherd, A. (2005) *Poverty and inequality in Britain*, London: Institute for Fiscal Studies.

Brighouse, T. (1996) 'Urban Deserts or Fine Cities', in M. Barber and R. Dann (eds) *Raising Educational Standards in the Inner Cities*. London: Cassell.

Burns, J. M. (1978) *Leadership*, NY: Harper & Row.

Castells, M. (2000) *End of Millenium*, Oxford: Blackwell.

Coffield, F. and Vignoles, A. (1997) *Widening Participation to Higher Education by Gender, Ethnicity and Age*, Report 5 of the National Committee of Inquiry into Higher Education. Norwich: HMSO.

Coffield, F. and Vignoles, A. (1997) 'Widening participation in higher education by ethnic minorities, women and alternative students' (Report 5) in National Committee of Inquiry into Higher Education, *Higher education in the learning society* (Dearing Report), London: HMSO.

Coffield, F., Moseley, D., Hall, E. and Ecclestone, K. (2004) *Should We Be Using Learning Styles? What Research Has to Say to Practice,* London: Learning Skills Research Centre.

Coleman, J.S., Campbell, E.Q., Hobson, C.J., McPartland, J., Mood, A.M., Wienfeld, F.D., and York, R.L. (1966) *Equality of Educational Opportunity*, Washington D.C.: Office of Education.

Crowther, D., Cummings, C., Dyson A. and Millward, A. (2003) *Schools and area regeneration,* York: JRF/The Policy Press.

Croxford, L. (2000) 'Inequality in Attainment at Age 16: A Home International Comparison', Paper delivered at CES conference. Centre for Educational Sociology, University of Edinburgh, 19 May.

Cullingford, C. and Daniels, S. (1998) 'The effects of Ofsted inspection on school performance', Huddersfield: University of Huddersfield.

Davies, B. and Ellison, L. (1996) *Strategic Marketing for Schools: How to Harmonise Marketing and Strategic Development for an Effective School,* London: Financial Times/Prentice Hall.

Davies, B. and Evans, J. (2001) 'Changing Cultures and Schools in England and Wales', in J. Cairns, D. Lawton and R. Gardner, *World Year Book of Education*, London: Kogan Page.

Davies, W. (2005) *Modernising with Purpose*: A Manifesto for a Digital Britain, London: Institute for Public Policy Research.

Delgado, M. (2002) *New Frontiers for Youth Development in the Twenty-first Century*, New York: Columbia University Press.

Department for Education and Science, (1965) The Organisation of Secondary Education (Circular 10/65).

Department for Education and Enterprise (1997) National Committee of Inquiry Inquiry into Higher Education *Higher education in the learning society* (Dearing Report), London: HMSO.

DES (1972) *Teacher Education and Training (The James Report)*, London: HMSO.

DfEE (2000) 'GCSE/GNVQ and GCE A/AS/Advanced GNVQ results for young people in England 1999/2000' Statistical First Release. http://dfes..gov.uk/rsgateway/DB/SFR/

DfEE (2001a) *Schools Building on Success*, Norwich: HMSO.

DfES (2001b) *Schools Achieving Success,* Annesley: DfES.

DfES (2001c) Press Release, http://www.dfes.gov.uk/pns

DfES (2002) *Neighbourhood Learning Centres: Case Study Pennywell Community Business (Sunderland)*, London: DfES.

DfES (2003) *Building schools for the future: Consultation on a new approach to capital investment*, London: DfES.

DfES (2004a) *Every Child Matters; Change for Children,* Outcomes framework, London: DfES.

DfES (2004b) *National Standards for Headteachers*, London: DfES.

DfES (2004c) *A New Relationship with Schools*, London: DfES

DfES (2005a) *14–19 Education and Skills,* Norwich: HMSO.

DfES (2005b) *Higher Standards, Better Schools For All: More choice for parents and pupils*, Norwich: HMSO.

DfES (2005c) *Extended schools: Access to opportunities and services for all. A prospectus,* London: DfES.

DfES (2006/1999) *Extending opportunity: a national framework for study support,* Nottingham: DfES.

Dodd, V. (2000) 'The Macpherson experience', 18 February, *Guardian*, http://www.guardian.co.uk/macpherson/article/0,,191684,00.html#article_continue

Dryfoos, J. (1994) *Full-Service Schools: A revolution in health and social services for children, youth and families*, San Francisco, CA: Jossey-Bass.

Dryfoos, J., Quinn, J. and Barkin C. (eds) (2005) *Community Schools In Action: Lessons From a Decade of Practice,* New York: Oxford University Press.

Earley, P., Baker, L. and Weindling, D., (1990) *Keeping the Raft Afloat: Secondary Headship Five Years On,* Slough: NFER.

Earley, P., Baker, L. and Weindling, D. (1995) Trapped in Post, *Managing Schools Today* (4) July.

Earley, P., Evans, J., Gold, A., Collarbone, P. and Halpin, D. (2002) *Establishing the Current State of School Leadership in England,* London: DfES.

Edwards, M. (2005) 'Civil society', *The Encyclopaedia of Informal Education*, www.infed.org/association/civil_society.htm.

Eisner, E. (2002) *The Arts and the Creation of Mind,* New Haven: Yale University Press.

Eisner, E. (2006) Speech in acceptance of lifetime award, American Educational Research Association, San Francisco, CA, 10 April.

Epstein J.L. (1992) 'School and Family Partnerships', in M. Alkin (ed.) *Encyclopedia of Educational Research* (6th edn), New York: Macmillan.

Epstein, J.L., Sanders, M. G., Simon, B. S., Salinas, K. C., Jansorn, N. R., and Van Voorhis, F. L. (2002) *School, family, and community partnerships: Your handbook for action* (2nd edn), Thousand Oaks, CA: Corwin.

ESRC data Society Today Fact Sheet http://www.esrc.ac.uk/ESRCInfoCentre/facts/index42.aspx?ComponentId=12640&SourcePageId=12719

Feinstein, L. and Symons, J. (1999) 'Attainment in secondary school', *Oxford Economic Papers*, 51, pp. 300–21.

Feinstein, L., Bynner, J. and Duckworth, K. (2005) *Leisure contexts in adolescence and their effects on adult outcomes*, London: University of London.

Field, J. (2003) *Social Capital*, London: Routledge.

Fink, D. (1999) 'The attrition of change', *International Journal of School Effectiveness and School Improvement* 10(3) 269–95.

Florian, L. and Rouse, M. (2001) Inclusive Practice in English Secondary Schools, *Cambridge Journal of Education,* 31(3), pp. 399–411.

Foster, A. (2005) *Realising their Potential: A Review of the Future Role of Further Education Colleges*, Nottingham: DfES.

Freire, P. (1970) *Pedagogy of the oppressed*, New York: Seabur.

Frost, D. (2005) 'Resisting the juggernaut: building capacity through teacher leadership in spite of it all', *Leading and Managing*, 10(2), pp. 70–87.

Fullan, M. (2000) 'The return of large-scale reforms', *Journal of Educational Change*, 2(1), pp. 5–28.

Gardner, H. (2003) 'Multiple Intelligences After Twenty Years', Paper presented at the American Educational Research Association Chicago IL, April 21, 2000.

Garner, R. (2006) 'Businesses told to think again about academy sponsorship', *Independent* 25 April.

General Teaching Council in Wales (GTCW) (2002) *Teacher Recruitment and Retention Survey*, Cardiff: General Teaching Council of Wales.

Gillborn, D. and Mirza, H. (2000) *Educational inequality: mapping race, class and gender,* London: Ofsted.

Gillborn, D. and Youdell, D. (2000) *Rationing Education: Policy, Practice, Reform and Equity*, Buckingham: Open University Press.

Good, R. (2006) 'ICT and self advocacy in students with severe learning difficulties', *Teacher Leadership*, 1(1), pp. 26–32.

Goodman, P. (1964) *Compulsory Miseducation*, London: Penguin.

Goodson, I. (1994) *Studying Curriculum: Cases and Methods*, Buckingham: Open University Press.

Gow, L. and McPherson. A. (1980) *Tell Them from Me,* Edinburgh: Centre for Educational Sociology.

Gray, J. (2000) *Causing Concern but Improving: A Review of Schools' Experiences*, Department for Education and Employment: Research Report RR188.

Gray, J. (2005) 'Some issues and problems in evaluating changes and improvements in "low performing" schools', in P. Clarke (ed.) *Improving Schools in Difficulty*, London: Continuum.

Goodman, P. (1964) *Compulsory Miseducation*, Harmondsworth, Middlesex: Penguin.

Gray, J. and Wilcox, B. (1995) *'Good School, Bad School': Evaluating Performance and Encouraging Improvement*, Buckingham: Open University Press.

Gray, J., Reynolds, D., Fitz-Gibbon, C. and Jesson, D. (eds) (1996) *Merging Traditions: The Future of Research on School Effectiveness and School Improvement*, London: Cassell.

Gray, J., Hopkins, D., Reynolds, D., Wilcox, B., Farrell, S. and Jesson, D. (1999) *Improving Schools: Performance and Potential*, Buckingham: Open University Press.

Green, H., McGinnity, A., Meltzer, H., Ford, T. and Goodman, R. (2005) *Mental health of children and young people in Great Britain, 2004: A survey carried out by the Office of National Statistics for the Department of Health and the Scottish Executive,* London: National Statistics.

Guardian (2006) The Wrigley Study, 22 May 2006. http://education.guardian.co.uk/newschools/story/0,,1780247,00.html.

Hargreaves D. H. (1967) *Social Relations in a Secondary School,* London: Routledge, Kegan Paul.

Hargreaves, D. H. (2003) 'Transformational learning', Talk given to the Leadership for Learning Project, Faculty of Education, University of Cambridge.

Hargreaves, D. (2004) *Personalised Learning: Next steps in Working Laterally*, London: Specialist Schools and Academies Trust.

Harlen, W. and Malcolm, H. (1999) *Setting and Streaming: A Research Review,* Edinburgh: Scottish Council for Research in Education.

Holt, J. ([1970] 2005) 'Schools are bad places for children', in *The Underachieving School* (revised and reprinted), Boulder, Colorado: Sentient Publications.

Hopkins, D. (2001) *School Improvement for Real*, London: RoutledgeFalmer.

Hopkins, D., West, M. and Ainscow, M. (1996) *Improving the Quality of Education for All: Progress and Challenge*, London: David Fulton.

Hopkins D., Beresford, J., Johnson, D., Sharpe, T., Singleton, C. and Watts, R. (2001) *Meeting the Challenge: An Improvement Gude for Schools Facing Challenging Circumstances,* Nottingham: University of Nottingham.

Hopkins, D., Beresford, J., and Sharpe, T. (2002) *Schools facing extremely challenging circumstances: Summary report of findings and conclusions September – December 2001*, Nottingham: University of Nottingham.

Hopkins, D., Reynolds, D. and Gray, J. (2005) *School Improvement – Lessons from Research*, London: DfES.

House of Commons Education and Skills Committee (2004) *Secondary Education: Teacher Retention and Recruitment Fifth Report of Session 2003–04,* vol I, HC 1057–I, London: The Stationery Office Limited.

House of Commons Select Committee on Education and Employment (1998) *Ninth Report to Parliament: The Role of Headteachers,* HC 725–I/725–II, London: The Stationery Office Ltd.

House of Commons (2005) *Select Committee on Education and Skills Fifth Report*, 9 March 2005.

House of Commons (2005) *Select Committee on Education and Skills Sixth Report*, London: House of Commons.

H. M. Government (2005) *Youth Matters*, London: The Stationery Office.

Howson, J. (2003) *The relationship between headteachers' length of service in primary and secondary schools and selected PANDA grades,* Nottingham: NCSL.

Illich, I. (1970) *Deschooling Society*, New York, NY: Harper and Row.

Imamdar, P. (2004) 'Computer skill development by children using "hole in the wall" facilties in rural India', *Australaisan Journal of Educational Technology*, 20(3), 337–50.

Independent (2005) Murdered head's school in academy row by Richard Garner, Education Editor. 25 November 2005. http://education.independent.co.uk/news/article 329178.ece.

Jencks, C.S., Smith, M., Ackland, H., Bane, M.J., Cohen, D., Gintis, H., Heyns, B. and Micholson, S. (1972) *Inequality: A Reassessment of the Effect of Family and Schooling in America*, New York: Basic Books.

Jesson, D. (2000) 'Evaluating Performance at GCSE in LEAs and Schools of Differing Types', York Centre for Performance Evaluation, February.

Johnston, R. and Watson, W. (2003) *Accelerating reading and spelling with synthetic phonics: a five year follow up*, Scottish Executive Education Department, Insight 4.

Kearns, A. and Parke, A. (2003) 'Living in and Leaving Poor Neighbourhood Conditions in England', *Housing Studies,* 18(6), pp. 827–51.

Kelly, R. Secretary of State for Education and Skills (2005a) 'Foreword' in *Higher Standards, Better Schools for All*.

Kelly, R. Secretary of State for Education and Skills (2005b) Speech to the Fabian Society; 30 March.

Kelly, R. Secretary of State for Education and Skills (2006) North of England Conference speech.

Kendall, L, O'Donnell, L., Golden, S., Ridley, K., Machin, S., Rutt, S., McNally, S., Schagen, I., Meghir, C., Stoney, S., Morris, M., West, A., and Noden, P. (2005) *Excellence in Cities: The National Evaluation of a Policy to Raise Standards in Urban Schools 2000–2003*. Research Report RR675A, Nottingham: DfES.

Kendall, L. and Schagen, I. (2004) *Excellence In Cities: Pupils' Performance At Key Stages 3 And 4*. Paper 18/2003 February 2004, http://www.nfer.ac.uk/publications/other-publications/downloadable-reports/pdf_docs/Paper182003.PDF.

Knapp, M., Copeland, M., Portin, B. and Plecki, M. (2006) 'Building Coherent Leadership "Systems" in Education: Roles, Resources, Information and Authority to Act'. Paper presented at the Annual Meeting of the American Educational Research Association, 7–11 April.

Kogan. M. (1987) 'The Plowden Report Twenty Years On' *Oxford Review of Education*, 13(1), 13–21.

Kozol, J. (1967) *Death at an Early Age*, London: Penguin Books.

Kozol, J. (1991) *Savage Inequalities*, New York: Crown Publishers.

Laming, Lord (2003) *The Victoria Climbié Inquiry, Report of an Inquiry by Lord Laming*. Speech by Lord Laming. Norwich: HMSO.

Lampl, Sir. Peter (2004) *Independent*, 24 June.

Lawrence-Lightfoot, S. (2003) *The Essential Conversation: What Parents and Teachers Can Learn from Each Other,* New York: Random House.

Learmonth, J. (2000) *Inspection: What's in it for schools?*, London: Routledge Falmer.

Levacic, R. (1994) *Local Management of Schools: analysis and practice*, Buckingham: Open University Press.

Lowe, R. (1867), Hansard, 1867

Lupton, R. (2004a) 'Do Poor Neighbourhoods mean Poor Schools?' Conference on 'Education and the Neighbourhood', in Bristol. London: Centre for Analysis of Social Exclusion, London School of Economics.

Lupton, R. (2004b) 'Schools in Disadvantaged Areas: Recognising Context and Raising Quality', London: Centre for Analysis of Social Exclusion, London School of Economics.

MacBeath, J., Galton, M., Steward, S., MacBeath, A., and Page C. (2006) *The Costs of Inclusion*, London: National Union of Teachers.

MacBeath, J., Kirwan, T., Myers, K., Smith, I., McCall, J. and Mackay, E. with Sharp, C., Bhabra, S., Pocklington, K., and Weindling, D. (2001) *The Impact of Study Support,* London: Department for Education and Skills.

MacBeath, J., Mearns, D. and Smith, M. (1986) *Home from School,* Glasgow: Jordanhill College.

MacBeath, J. and Mortimore, P. (eds) (2001) *Improving School Effectiveness*, Buckingham: Open University Press.

MacGilchrist, B. (2003) *Has school improvement passed its sell-by date?* London: Institute of Education, University of London.

Maden, M. (ed.) (2001) *Success Against the Odds: Five Years On – Revisiting Effective Schools in Disadvantaged Areas*, London: RoutledgeFalmer.

Mangan, J., Gray, J. and Pugh, G. (2005) 'Changes in examination performance in English secondary schools over the course of a decade: searching for patterns and trends over time', *School Effectiveness and School Improvement*, 16(1), pp. 29–50.

Matthews, P. and Sammons, P. (2004) *Improvement through Inspection: an evaluation of the impact of Ofsted's work*, London: Ofsted.

Mckenley, J. (2005) *Developing Community Leaders Report: 04/05*, Nottingham: NCSL.

McLuhan, M. (1967) *The Medium is the Message*, New York: Random House.

McPherson, A. and Willms, J.D. (1987) 'Equalisation and improvement: some effects of comprehensive re-organisation in Scotland', *Sociology,* 21, pp. 509–39.

Mendel, M. (2003) 'The Space that Speaks' in S. Castelli, M. Mendel and B. Ravn, (eds) *School, Family and Community Partnerships in a World of Differences and Changes*, Gdansk: Wydawnicto Uniwersytetu Gdanskiego.

Mental Health Foundation (2005) *Lifetime Impacts: Childhood and Adolescent Mental Health: Understanding the lifetime impacts*, London: Mental Health Foundation.

Miliband, D. (2003) 'Workforce reform: no turning back', 17 June, *Guardian*:

Miliband, D. (2004) Personalised learning: building a new relationship with schools. Speech by David Miliband, Minister of State for School Standards North of England Education conference, Belfast, 8 January.

Ministry of Education (1960) *The Youth Service in England and Wales* ('The Albemarle Report'), London: Her Majesty's Stationery Office.

Mirza, H. (2005) 'The more things change, the more they stay the same: assessing Black underachievement 35 years on', in Richardson, B. (ed.) *Tell It Like It Is: How our Schools Fail Black Children,* Stoke on Trent: Trentham Books.

Mitra, M. and Rana, V. (2001) 'Children and the Internet: Experiments with Minimally Invasive Education in India', *British Journal of Educational Technology*, 32(2), pp. 221–32.

Morris, H. (1925) *The Village College. Being a Memorandum on the Provision of Educations and Social Facilities for the Countryside, with Special Reference to Cambridgeshire*, Cambridge: Cambridge University Press.

Mortimore, P. (2006) *Which Way Forward?,* London: National Union of Teachers.

Mulford, B. (2003) *School Leaders: Changing Roles and Impact on Teacher and School Effectiveness,* Paris: OECD.

National Audit Office (2006) *Improving Poorly Performing Schools in England*, London: The Stationery Office.

National Commission on Education (1995) *Success Against the Odds*, London: Routledge and Kegan Paul.

National Commission on Education (1996) *Success against the odds: effective schools in disadvantaged areas*, London: Routledge.

National Statistics http://www.statistics.gov.uk/

National Union of Teachers (2005) *Bringing Down the Barriers* NUT education statement: meeting the needs of all children and young people, London: NUT.

Newsom Report (1963) Public Schools Commission First Report, Half Our Future. London: HMSO.

ODPM (2004) *The English Indices of Deprivation* (rev.), Wetherby: ODPM

OECD (2001) *Knowledge and Skills for Life: First results from PISA 2000*, Paris: OECD.

OECD (2003) *Student Engagement at School: A Sense of Belonging and Participation: Results from PISA 2000*, Paris OECD.

OECD (2004) *Learning for Tomorrow's World: First Results from PISA 2003*, Paris: OECD.

Office for Standards in Education (2005) *The Annual Report of Her Majesty's Chief Inspector of Schools*, London, Ofsted.

Ofsted (1997) *From Failure to Success: How Special Measures are Helping Schools to Improve*, London: Ofsted.

Ofsted (2002) *Achievement of Black Caribbean Pupils: Good Practice in Secondary Schools*, London: Ofsted.

Ofsted (2005) *Every Child Matters: Framework for the Inspection of Schools in England from 2005,* London: Ofsted.

Orfield, G. (1998) *Chilling Admissions: The Affirmative Action Crisis and the Search for Alternatives*, Boston, MA: Harvard Education Publishing Group.

Owen, D., Green, A., Pitcher, J. and Maguire, M. (2000) *Minority ethnic participation and achievements in education, training and the labour market*, Research Report No. 225, Norwich: HMSO.

Palmer, G., Carr, J., and Kenway P. (2005) *Monitoring poverty and social exclusion 2005* York: JRF/New Policy Institute.

Parliamentary Select Committee for Communities and Local Government http://www.publications.parliament.uk/pa/cm/cmcomloc.htm

Perkins, D, (2004) *Making Thinking Visible*, Cambridge, MA: Harvard Graduate School of Education.

Pinker, S. (1998) *Words and Rules*, Brattleborough, VT: Lingua.

Pinker, S. (1999) *How the Mind Works*, New York: W.W. Norton.

Plowden, Lady (chair) (1967) *Children and their Primary Schools*, London: HMSO.

Prime Minister's Office (2003) Prime Minister's speech on the launch of the Children's Green Paper, *Every Child Matters*, www.number-10.gov.uk/output/Page4426.asp.

Putnam, R. D. (2000) *Bowling Alone: The Collapse and Revival of American Community*, New York: Simon and Schuster.

Qualifications and Curriculum Authority (QCA) (2006) *The Curriculum: QCA Looks Forward*. London: QCA.

Qvortrup, L. (2001) *Det lærende samfund* [*The Learning Society*], København: Gyldendal.

Ranson, S. (2000) Recognising the pedagogy of voice in a learning community, *Educational Management and Administration,* 28, 3, 263–79.

Reynolds, D., Hopkins, D., Potter, D. and Chapman, C. (2001a) 'School Improvement for Schools Facing Exceptionally Challenging Circumstances: A Review of the Literature', Paper prepared for the Regional Conferences for Schools Facing Challenging Circumstances, London: Department for Education and Employment.

Reynolds, D., Hopkins, D., Potter, D. Chapman, C. (2001b) *School Improvement for Schools Facing Challenging Circumstances: A Review of Research and Practice*, //www.standards.dfes.gov.uk/sie/si/SfCC/.

Robbins Commission (1963) *Higher Education Report of the Committee Appointed By the Prime Minister Under the Chairmanship of Lord Robbins 1961–63,* London: HMSO, Committee on Higher Education.

Rose, J., (2006) *Independent Review of the Teaching of Early Reading,* Nottingham: DfES

Rosenthal, L. (2001). 'The cost of regulation in education: do school inspections improve school quality?' Department of Economics, University of Keele, p.16.

Rosenthal, L. (2004) Do school inspections improve school quality? Ofsted inspections and school examination results in the UK, *Economics of Education Review,* 23, 1, pp. 143–151.

Rudduck, J. and Flutter, J. (2004) *How to Improve Your School: Giving pupils a voice*, London: Continuum.

Rutter, M., Maughan, B., Mortimore, P. and Ouston, J. (1979) *Fifteen Thousand Hours: Secondary Schools and Their Effects on Children*, London: Open Books.

Sammons, P., Power, S., Elliott, K., Robertson, P., Campbell, C. and Whitty, G. (2003) *New Community Schools in Scotland: Final Report (National Evaluation of the Pilot Phase)*, London: Institute of Education.

School of Barbiana (1969) *Letter to a Teacher*, London: Penguin.

Scottish Executive (2004) *Guidance for Community Learning and Development Working and learning together to build stronger communities*, Edinburgh: Scottish Executive.

Sharp, C., Blackmore, J., Kendall, L., Schagen, I., Mason, K. and O'Connor, K. (2002) *Playing for Success: an evaluation of the third year*, Norwich: National Foundation for Educational Research / Department for Education and Skills, HMSO.

Shaw, I., Newton, D.P., Aitken, M. and Darnell, R. (2003) Do Ofsted inspections of secondary schools make a difference in GCSE results?, *British Educational Research Journal*, 29, 1, pp. 62–75.

Simon, B. (1981) 'Why no pedagogy in England?', in B. Simon and W. Taylor (eds.) *Education in the Eighties: the central issues*, London: Batsford.

Smith, M. K. (2005) Extended schooling – some issues for informal and community education', *The Encyclopedia of Informal Education*, www.infed.org/schooling/extended_schooling. htm. Last updated: June 24, 2005.

Smith, M. K. (2005) 'Youth Matters – The Green Paper for Youth 2005', *The Encyclopaedia of Informal Education*, www.infed.org/youth work/green_paper.htm.

Spencer, H. (1861) *Essays on Education and Kindred Subjects*, London: Dent.

Spillane, J. P. (2006) *Distributed Leadership*, San Francisco CA, Jossey-Bass.

Stoll, L, Fink, D. and Earl, L. (2003) *It's About Learning (and It's About Time)*, London: RoutledgeFalmer.

Stoll, L. and Myers, K. (eds) (1998) *No Quick Fixes: Perspectives on Schools in Difficulty*, London, Falmer Press.

Stubbs, Lady Marie (2006) BBC broadcast, 29 July.

Surowiecki, J. (2004) *The Wisdom of Crowds*, New York: Random House.

Swaffield, S. and MacBeath, J. (2005) Self-evaluation and the role of the critical friend, *Cambridge Journal of Education*, 35: pp. 259–93.

Taylor C. (2001) 'Hierarchies and "local" markets: the geography of the "lived" market place in secondary education provision', *Journal of Education Policy*, 16(3), pp. 197– 214.

Teddlie, C. and Reynolds, D. (eds) (2000) *The International Handbook of School Effectiveness Research*, London: Falmer Press.

The Sutton Trust (2006) *The Social Composition of Top Comprehensive Schools: Rates of Eligibility for Free School Meals at the 200 Highest Performing Comprehensive Schools*, www.suttontrust.com.

Thomas, S., Gray, J. and Peng, W.J. (in press) Value-added trends in English secondary school performance over ten years, *Oxford Review of Education*.

Thrupp, M. (1999) *Schools Making a Difference: Let's be Realistic! School mix, school effectiveness and the social limits of reform*, Buckingham: Open University Press.

Tomlinson, M. et al. (2004) 14–19 *Curriculum and Qualifications Reform: Final Report of the Working Group on 14–19 Reform*, Nottingham: DfES.

University of Queensland (2004) *Home, School and Community Partnerships to support children's numeracy*, Department of Education, Science and Training, University of Queensland.

Vignoles, A., Galindo-Rueda, F. and Marcenaro-Gutierrez, O. (2004) 'The widening socio-economic gap in UK higher education', *National Institute Economic Review*, 190, pp. 70–82.

Wall, K., Higgins, S. and Smith, H. (2005) ' "The visual helps me understand the complicated things": pupil views of teaching and learning with interactive whiteboards', *British Journal of Educational Technology*, 36(5), pp. 851–67.

Wallace, M. (1993) 'Discourse of derision: the role of the mass media in the educational policy process', *Journal of Educational Policy,* 8(4), pp. 321–37.

Warnock, M. (2005) *Special educational needs: a new look*, No. 11 in a series of policy discussions. Published by the Philosophy of Education Society of Great Britain.

Webster, C., Simpson, D., MacDonald, R., Abbas, A., Cieslik, M., Shildrick T., and Simpson, M. (2004) *Poor transitions: Social exclusion and young adults*, Bristol: Policy Press.

Weiss, L. and Fine, M. (eds) (2000) *Construction Sites: Excavating Race, Class and Gender among Urban Youth*, New York: Teachers College Press.

White, J. (ed.) (2004) *Rethinking the school curriculum.* London: RoutledgeFalmer.

Wilkin, A., Kinder, K., White, R., Atkinson, M. and Doherty, P. (2003) *Towards the Development of Extended Schools*, Slough: NFER.

Willis, P. (1977) *Learning to Labour. How working-class kids get working-class jobs,* London: Gower.

Wolf, A. (2002) *Does Education Matter?: myths about education and economic growth*, London: Penguin.

Wolfendale, S. (1992) *Empowering parents and teachers: working for children,* London: Cassell.

World Health Organisation (2005) http://www.who.int/mediacentre/news/releases/2004/pr61/en/

Wrigley, T. (2006) *Another School is Possible,* Stoke-on-Trent: Trentham Books.

Wylie, T. (2004) Address to the Leadership for Learning Cambridge Network, Cambridge, April.

Wyse, D. (2003) The National Literacy Strategy: A Critical Review of Empirical Evidence, *British Educational Research Journal*. Vol. 29 (6): 903–16.

Youdell, D. (2003) 'Identity traps or how black students fail: the interactions between biographical, sub-cultural, and learner identities', *British Journal of Sociology of Education*, 24(1), pp. 4–20.

Youth Matters, (2005) DfES, Norwich: HMSO.

Index